AGORAPHOBIA

Explains the background causes of the phobia, and
demonstrates that relief and cure are possible. Includes
self-help advice.

In the same series
DEPRESSION
  Dr Caroline Shreeve
DIVORCE
  Dr Caroline Shreeve

AGORAPHOBIA

Coping with the World Outside

by

Muriel Frampton
M.Th., B.Com.

TURNSTONE PRESS LIMITED
Wellingborough, Northamptonshire

First published in 1974 as *Overcoming Agoraphobia*
This edition completely revised and reset August 1984
Second Impression August 1984

British Library Cataloguing in Publication Data

Frampton, Muriel
   Agoraphobia.—Completely rev. and reset ed.
   1. Agoraphobia—Treatment
   I. Title   II. Frampton, Muriel.   Overcoming
   agoraphobia
   616.85'225   RC535

   ISBN 0-85500-213-1

*Turnstone Press is part of the
Thorsons Publishing Group*

Printed and bound in Great Britain

CONTENTS

	Page
Foreword	7
Introduction	9
Chapter	
PART I: UNDERSTANDING	13
1. What is Agoraphobia?	15
2. The Symptoms of Agoraphobia	21
3. Precipitating Causes	26
4. What is the *Real* Cause?	30
5. Agoraphobia and Claustrophobia	39
PART II: THE WAY FORWARD	45
6. Freedom from Fear	47
7. Behaviour Therapy	52
8. Is It Necessary to Find the Cause?	58
9. Analytic Psychotherapy	62
10. Methods of Self-help	66
11. Resistance	78

12. What About My Children?   82

13. Over to You   86

     Useful Addresses   91

     Further Reading   93

     Index   95

FOREWORD

No more important discovery for the welfare of mankind has emerged in this century than psychoanalysis. But so far only a tiny fraction of the population has come within reach of its benefits. It is relatively unrecognized. By far the great majority of our overworked psychiatrists in the National Health Service, though appreciative of Freud's work, are not trained in psychoanalysis, and at present there exists a wide gap between this highly expensive yet invaluable treatment, and the numberless thousands of ordinary men and women who desperately need it.

As far as agoraphobia is concerned, it is this gap that this present volume seeks to span. Written in homely sympathetic style, it opens the ordinary sufferer's eyes to the true causes of his crushing malady, encourages deep insight, and so makes possible relief and even cure.

In contrast to the orthodox psychiatric approach to the problem of agoraphobia, Muriel Frampton embarks on an effort to explain in easy everyday language the deep unconscious motivations that produce this widespread illness. Alas, too many psychiatrists — because of lack of time or training — treat the symptoms of this handicap either by drugs or by a series of 'behaviourist' contrivances, designed to jockey the sufferer into a situation where he — or she — forgets to be afraid. These manipulations of personality may help some sufferers and bring elements of relief, but they do not lay the foundations of a more adequate personality liberated from further flights into agoraphobia.

The author of this book rightly emphasizes that she is not seeking merely to eliminate this or that *symptom*, still less to encourage the patient to tolerate or 'live with it' but, by understanding on a deep level, to make possible the growth of a more adequate self with which to face life and its challenges.

If you are a victim of phobias, do not treat this book as a magic wand for instant relief. This book conceals as well as reveals valuable analytic insights. Only as you read it over and over again, mark passages in it that 'ring bells' in your mind, and work consistently on its suggestions, will you come to enjoy the release it offers.

One word about the author. Handicapped in infancy by poliomyelitis which left her with a permanent limp, she faced life bravely and soon gave evidence of marked versatility. Apart from graduating in the contrasting fields of economics and divinity she also became an Associate of Trinity College, London, and a Licentiate of the Royal Academy of Music. For years she lectured in economics and accountancy, then, still unsatisfied, she subjected herself to a rigorous psychoanalytic training for her present vocation as a psychotherapist, because in so doing, she felt she could best help suffering people. The quality of her understanding and dedication shines out in this book as it does in her psychotherapeutic practice. I commend the book heartily.

C. Edward Barker

INTRODUCTION

Only those who suffer from agoraphobia, or live with someone afflicted in this way, know the misery involved.

A person who has lived a successful life, shouldered responsibilities, and travelled about quite freely may suddenly, for no apparent reason, become a victim of fear. He, or she, begins to tremble like a leaf at the prospect of having to make a short journey, and may not even be able to get as far as the garden gate without being overwhelmed by panic. It all seems so inexplicable.

The distress of the patient is aggravated by the knowledge that the rest of the family are suffering as well. The mother who cannot see her daughter receive her award at the school prize-giving, or her son play the lead in *Hamlet*, blames herself for their obvious disappointment.

The holiday season is a nightmare. Other youngsters go on outings and away for holidays with their parents. The mother who is a victim of agoraphobia is very much aware of this, and for the sake of the children she tries to be brave, and says she will go. But just at the last minute she may be utterly defeated and in a flood of tears.

If her husband is in a good position, in the type of work which demands some sharing of social life, she feels that she is letting him down, and involving him in giving awkward explanations, by her inability to accompany him.

What is more, the family just don't seem to understand,

which is not surprising seeing that the patient does not know what has happened either. It is all so bewildering and appears to be hopeless. How can you put something right, when you do not really know what is wrong?

It is the purpose of this book to help those who suffer like this, and to help their families, by:

1. Explaining the 'inexplicable' — pointing to possible, and indeed probable, causes of the trouble.
2. Indicating the forms of professional help available.
3. Making suggestions for self-help.

Regarding the last point, I am particularly bearing in mind the fact that the agoraphobic patient is, by definition, one who cannot easily travel to a professional psychotherapist. It may therefore be necessary for him, or her, to practise self-help — in the early stages at least.

It is *not* my purpose here, to give practical advice and suggestions about 'living with' agoraphobia — that is, making life more tolerable and interesting within the context of the restrictions suffered by the patient. As a therapist, it is my primary aim to work for healing. This does not mean that I am unaware of the need for interim help with practical problems. These vary so much from one patient to another, however, that I feel the particular needs of individuals can best be met through personal contact of some kind.

Phobics' Societies

It is partly in answer to this situation that various societies have been formed, both in this country and abroad, to cater for the needs of phobics. The reasons are, I think, not hard to find: most agoraphobes seek anonymity, yet find great relief in talking to others who have had the same problem and are indeed relieved to find that they are not alone in their difficulties. The lack of insight and knowledge among some GPs has forced agoraphobics to form their own organizations for mutual help and exchange of information; a lack of sympathy from the family has the same effect.

In particular, those who have suffered from agoraphobia and found a way through it have much to offer to others in the same plight. So it was that The Open Door organization was formed in 1965 by Mrs Alice Neville, and is still thriving under its present secretary, Mrs Mona Woodford.

The Phobics Society was founded by Katherine Fisher, someone who likewise triumphed over immense difficulties and came to realize that she could help others who were still struggling and needed support.

Both of these societies number their members in thousands and, along with other groups, offer somewhat similar help. The Phobics Society in particular aims to help by:

1. Giving immediate advice and understanding to those who desperately seek help — an essential 'first-aid' service.
2. Convincing sufferers that they are not 'freaks' but have a well-documented illness which can be treated and overcome.
3. Setting up branches throughout the country to allow phobics to discuss their problem and exchange views.
4. Arranging tangible help, wherever possible, for those who are alone and totally incapacitated by their illness.
5. Disseminating any new and helpful information relating to phobic illness and its treatment.
6. Keeping up constant pressure on the appropriate central government and local government departments to give greater recognition to and to take action on the plight of phobics in the U.K.

There is always the danger, of course, that people may use such societies as a crutch, rather than a means of finding release from the phobia. One person, writing about The Open Door, has said: 'Don't join if you want to wallow in your symptoms and feed your self-pity.' That is sound advice.

There is, nevertheless, a need for the patient to be able to talk to someone who is sympathetic; and for people who live alone or whose family cannot help, the friendship and understanding of a fellow-sufferer can be a boon.

You will find the addresses of several phobics societies at the end of this book.

PART I
UNDERSTANDING

1.

WHAT IS AGORAPHOBIA?

A 'phobia' is a fear which a person knows to be irrational and exaggerated, but which he simply cannot control. For example, a man who is otherwise quite tough may turn green at the thought of going up in an aeroplane. You may tell him that far more people are killed on the roads than in air crashes. It will make no difference. He cannot reason himself out of the fear.

There are very many different kinds of phobias — over 200 have been listed, but the list is incomplete. Some are well known: phobias about mice, spiders, snakes, thunder and lightning, and public speaking are not uncommon, to mention only a few. Perhaps you know someone who has a fear of heights (acrophobia); and most people have heard of claustrophobia — the fear of enclosed spaces.

Yet the term 'agoraphobia' was almost unknown until two or three decades ago. People who were afraid to venture out from their homes were just thought of as peculiar. At first, perhaps they received sympathy, but as their condition persisted or worsened their families became irritated and critical, or tried with kind intentions to laugh (or bully) them out of it. Their trouble was neither understood, nor recognized for what it was. Nor was it realized just how many suffer from this affliction.

The Term 'Agoraphobia'

The word 'agoraphobia' is derived from two Greek words —
phobos meaning 'fear', and *agora* meaning 'a place of assembly,
or market-place'. It is, then, the 'fear of public places'. The
victims of the phobia describe it in different ways, according
to their own symptoms. One will say it is the 'fear of open
spaces' while another says it is a 'fear of crowds', or a 'fear of
leaving home'.

Agoraphobes (as such people are called) are by no means
rare, so if you are a victim of this fear you must not think you
are alone and peculiar in your predicament. There are all too
many who suffer from this phobia: it is estimated, in fact, that
there are about half a million agoraphobes in the country today.

People Affected in Different Ways

Patients vary enormously in the degree to which their lives
are handicapped by the phobia. One person is able to go out
fairly happily provided she is in the company of someone else.
Another woman is unable to leave the house at all; as soon as
she gets outside the garden gate she feels dizzy and faint. Her
legs seem just like jelly, and she retreats in panic to her front
door and shuts herself in once more.

A young mother once told me how for a time she really felt
safe only *in bed*, and in fact spent the major part of her days
in the bedroom.

Recently one man spoke to me of his wife's dilemma. 'She
appears to be a perfectly normal person', he said. 'You'd never
think there was anything wrong with her. But she cannot walk
across a street alone. Yet she can *drive* anywhere. In fact, she
is a marvellous driver. I just cannot understand it.'

A young man came to me for help with the opposite problem:
he could go out and about fairly freely, but felt quite unsafe
when driving his car, especially on a broad, straight road like
a motorway.

The problem of one young wife, severely agoraphobic,
centres around her fear of being seen. She is willing to go into
the garden to play with the children, but on no account will
she have her photograph taken with them — not even if she
herself is in the house, looking at them through a window.

There are countless different ways in which individuals are
affected. The *width* of the street is often significant. One person
may be terrified of venturing into a wide street, while another

is equally fearful of a narrow one. A sudden *change* of width is nearly always upsetting.

In some cases the phobia gets such a hold that it becomes not only a fear of going out, but a dread of being alone, even in the house. The whole of life, in fact, becomes fraught with fear and panic. There is a desperate need to make contact, and life becomes almost impossible without the daily phone call to one's mother or daughter, or a friend.

The Need For a Way of Escape

The agoraphobe fears especially those situations in which he feels he has no way of escape. For this reason if he *does* go to a theatre or cinema he makes sure he can get a gangway seat. At any social gatherings he will find a seat near the door.

Only with the greatest reluctance will such a person board a bus, and if he does, he will likewise sit or stand near the door. An injunction to 'move down the bus, please' will cause him to tremble like a leaf, and he may well murmur some excuse to get off the bus before he has reached his destination, rather than suffer the agonies of the situation.

One man could drive his own car quite cheerfully, but whenever he was a passenger in any vehicle driven by another person he would break out in a sweat, because he was not free to stop the vehicle when he wanted. He felt trapped.

Similarly, journeys abroad are definitely out, for one cannot get off a ship or plane just when a fit of panic strikes!

It can be seen that life becomes very restricted indeed when once the phobia gets a hold, and not infrequently the patient ends up by not going out of the house at all.

The Prevalence of the Phobia

One of the reasons why agoraphobia is so prevalent (it is estimated that eight to ten people in every thousand of the population suffer from it) is that almost any phobia may be quickly translated into a fear of going out. If you are afraid of cats, for example, you dread going out in case you see one. If you have a phobia about receiving infection, you will soon reach the point of staying indoors. It has been estimated that over fifty per cent of all phobics suffer from agoraphobia as one of their symptoms.

Unfortunately, when once the fear of going out has established itself, its hold on the sufferer tends to become more and more firm. Why is this? One of the reasons is that staying in the house is a habit that is formed very easily, almost unconsciously, and may get a hold before one realizes it.

The Phobia of Every Day
In the case of some phobias, the situation can be avoided for the most part, or it arises only occasionally. For instance, it is not every day that one sees a mouse, much less a snake. A person who is afraid of heights can generally avoid the situations in which he would find himself in a panic. The man who is terrified of flying may be able to use other means of transport.

The agoraphobe, on the other hand, is *continually* made aware of his difficulty. He has to contend with his phobia every single day — and if he gives into it, it very soon becomes firmly entrenched.

It Has To Be Faced in Public
Whereas one can attempt to overcome some types of fear in the privacy of one's own home, or in the company of friends, in the nature of the case agoraphobia can only be overcome by venturing out in public, and facing the possibility of a panic in public. Now this is a very different matter, because it is, in fact, the very core of the fear.

Indeed one writer has suggested that agoraphobia is wrongly named. It is not, he says, 'fear of public places' but the 'fear of being afraid'. By this he means that agoraphobes are not afraid of the street, or the bus or train, as such. Rather, they are afraid of being overwhelmed by fear in such places, where they are unable to find supportive help. It is the *panic* in a public place which they dread.

In this way the phobia is perpetuated. For it is one thing to make a brave attempt to overcome a fear in private: it is quite another to risk embarrassment in a public place.

Women More Than Men
Any person may become the victim of a phobia, but it is interesting to find that ninety per cent of phobic patients are women. Certainly it is true that agoraphobia, in particular, is much more common among women than men. You may wonder why this is, and I would suggest several contributory factors.

In the first place, a man normally has little choice but to go out and earn a living. There are few jobs which he is likely to do at home. This means that the habit does not so easily get a chance to become established. Despite the anxiety he suffers, he is forced to make the effort.

Moreover, his weakness is readily apparent if he remains at home and leaves his wife to go out to earn a living for both of them. He would be embarrassed by such an arrangement, so he has a strong incentive to face his fear, and put up with the difficulty he experiences.

A woman on the other hand is usually in a different situation. Indeed she can actually fulfil herself in the home to a much greater extent than is possible for her husband. A man tied to the house will probably get so bored that he will make every effort to go out. In doing this he is also helping himself, for as he faces his fear it will lessen rather than increase. I shall have more to say on that in a later chapter.

Secondly — despite the Women's Lib movement — the social climate probably still tends to boost the male ego rather than the female. For example, many parents are especially pleased when they are blessed with a boy, and this is particularly true of the mother, on whom a baby is more dependent for acceptance at the very beginning of life. It is no mere coincidence that ego-weakness, one of the contributory factors in agoraphobia, is found more generally in women than in men.

Thirdly, it is also probably true that frustration of sexual desire is more common among women than among men. The reasons for this lie partly in their differing attitudes to sex and promiscuity, partly in the imbalance of sex distribution in certain age groups, and in many other factors. Agoraphobia which stems from a sexual conflict (as it does in *some* cases) is therefore more likely to affect women.

On the Increase

It does seem that agoraphobia is more prevalent today than it used to be. One must remember, of course, that only in recent years, since the phobia has been recognized and treated, have many people come forward for help. In the past there have been many cases (and indeed there still are) which are quite unknown to the people who compile statistics. Such folk have retired into their homes and confided their problems to very few people; their distress remains a private matter and there is no record of their illness.

It is well-known, however, that symptoms of nervous strain and tension *are* more prevalent today than ever before, and no doubt the incidence of agoraphobia reflects this general trend.

2.

THE SYMPTOMS OF AGORAPHOBIA

The physical effects vary from person to person, but certain symptoms are commonly experienced during an 'attack'. Giddiness often occurs, along with palpitations or difficulty in breathing. Unfortunately, if you suffer like this you may fear that there is something physically wrong with you, and this increases the panic. You become even *more* reluctant to go far from home in case you have an attack.

In actual fact you are probably perfectly healthy, but in any case it is better to have a check-up with your doctor, than refuse to go out for fear that you may have a heart attack. When you know you are in good health, you can tackle the *real* reasons for your fear, which are emotional.

Another common symptom is the feeling that one's legs just will not function. Either they feel wobbly (jelly-legs is quite an apt description), or they feel as heavy as lead, with no freedom of movement in them. Again it is important to realize that this 'weakness' is only a natural result of tension and stress. It is not an indication of some physical defect.

The same thing applies to many other symptoms felt by agoraphobes and nervous sufferers generally. Choking feelings, sweating, headaches, 'churning' of the stomach — these are quite usual accompaniments of tension, though I will not embark here on an explanation of the biological reasons for them.

If you suffer in this way, it may help if you remember that

every one of us has known something of these symptoms in times of stress.

The nervous speaker, for instance, finds his mouth becomes so dry just before he is called on to deliver his address, that he rapidly takes a glass of water if it is available. Even so he may wonder whether he can manage to get the words out.

The music student is dismayed when her hands start to tremble and perspire as she waits her turn to play before the examiners.

Which of us has not experienced 'butterflies' in the stomach when we have attended some important interview or performed at some public function?

Such symptoms are a *perfectly normal* outcome of tension, and generally we manage to put up with them because we know that they are only temporary and will disappear as soon as the cause of the stress is past.

Unfortunately, to the victim of agoraphobia these physical discomforts cause not merely temporary embarrassment but panic and hysterical anxiety and, not infrequently, a flood of tears.

Overwhelmed

Apart from the physical symptoms of stress, many agoraphobes suffer from an awful dread of being overwhelmed, and from feelings of unreality which can be very frightening.

A young student told me how, on returning to college after one vacation, she had just this experience. If she went into a crowded store, or even into a busy street she felt quite overwhelmed by the crowds and the traffic. She did not even want to be with her own group of friends. It was all too much for her. There was an awful feeling of unreality which terrified her, and she was thankful that a short course of relaxation treatment put her right again.

More General Characteristics

Indecision is something which plagues *many* nervous sufferers — not to mention their families! This is particularly so in the case of the agoraphobic patient, who tends to be courageous and optimistic one day, and is then overcome by fear and despair the next. She may want to see a particular production at the local theatre, and be determined to make the effort. Her husband gets the tickets in advance, thinking it will encourage her, but at the very last minute she finds she cannot face it.

Holidays are an even greater problem, as bookings have to be made so long in advance and the payment of a deposit is often involved. There are the children to consider too. They are too young and full of spirits to understand their mother's difficulty. They feel let down, and this only piles on the agony for the mother who feels guilty and responsible for their disappointment.

Little Initiative

The agoraphobe who cannot make her own decisions often ends up by falling in with whatever other people suggest. She has no confidence in herself to take the initiative in anything, and appears apathetic and lacking in interest. Indeed, she *is* apathetic very often, for any kind of prolonged nervous stress is debilitating. So much energy goes into dealing with the emotional struggle that one's reserves are depleted. There is little joy or excitement in life. One's whole existence becomes a battle against fear, apathy, guilt and depression.

Again so much depends on the individual's own background and temperament. I know of one young mother who appears to accept her restricted life quite happily, as long as no one tries to bully her to go out. If she can be left alone to do as she likes she seems to be perfectly content. I am not, however, commending this 'acceptance' as the right solution to the problem. The aim, for the sake of both the sufferer and his/her family, must be to go forward to find release.

Aggressiveness

Many agoraphobic patients find themselves somewhat short-tempered and aggressive with the family, and with friends who try to help them.

The general complaint behind it all is: 'You just don't understand'. As I have said before, this is indeed true. The phobia is quite bewildering to other people as well as to the patient and, what is more, the family is involved in the effects of it.

If you suffer an accident and find yourself in hospital, or if you become seriously ill, you may receive lots of sympathy, get-well cards and loving attention from the family.

But this is different. You are involving your family in your suffering, and because they can see no good reason for it, they resent it. Or they try to chivvy you out of it — which *you* resent.

Their lack of understanding is hard to bear, and serves to increase your difficulty. You feel guilty on the one hand, yet you feel hurt and badly used, even spiteful about it all. Moreover, the state of tension in which you so often find yourself makes you edgy and nervy — ready to fly off the handle quickly. So now you have a second source of guilt — your own aggression.

Strained Relationships

Unfortunately, as the agoraphobic patient becomes more and more withdrawn into his, or her, restricted life, relationships easily become strained. A couple who used to be very happy together may be driven apart, each blaming the other for a lack of understanding. The husband may come to feel that his wife is not prepared to *try* to overcome her trouble and share life with him as she used to do, while the wife may be so preoccupied with her daily fight against feelings of terror and panic that she can no longer be 'outward looking'. She becomes introspective and (understandably) concerned primarily for herself. Every morning she wakes up with only one thought in her mind: how to 'get through the day'. This constant struggle absorbs so much of her inner resources that she can raise little interest in the affairs of other people.

This is the situation at its worst, but happily things are not always as bad as that. Sometimes the sufferer is blessed with a very understanding partner, who is prepared to be patient and loving. In other cases the agoraphobe is not so withdrawn as this, and can enter imaginatively and sympathetically into the life of the other members of the family.

Intolerance

Patients who are severely agoraphobic often display another characteristic trait: an intolerance of other people's difficulties. It may seem strange that patients who so often complain of a lack of understanding of their own problems should be unsympathetic towards the sufferings of other people.

Yet agoraphobes tend to regard other phobias as far less debilitating and agonizing than their own fearful state. There may be some justification for this, but it is also true that one has to experience the difficulties of another person to know what can be involved. The Open Door organization once reported having received letters from some two hundred people suffering from spider phobia, which revealed that it could be almost as crippling as agoraphobia.

Even within the ranks of agoraphobes one finds people who are 'jealous' about the use of the term 'agoraphobia'. Someone who is not *totally* unable to go out may be told he does not really suffer from agoraphobia at all!

Another interesting fact reported by The Open Door is that ex-agoraphobes can sometimes be very intolerant of those who are still victims of the phobia. This seems even more strange. No doubt it is easy for those who have 'won through' to see others as weak, but one must remember that some cases are more severe and more complex than others.

So much depends upon the degree to which the phobia restricts the person. Some patients are caught up in a general state of chronic anxiety, of which agoraphobia is just one manifestation. They suffer exaggerated fears in almost any situation, not just in the matter of going out of the house. There are others who show scarcely any abnormality except in one particular regard — say, crossing a road alone.

Many agoraphobes suffer from claustrophobia in certain situations, and this will be dealt with in a later chapter.

So much for the symptoms of agoraphobia. They add up to a great deal of misery, for the victim most of all, but also for members of the family, whose social life becomes more difficult and restricted.

Is there a way out? Fortunately there is. In the following chapters we shall be looking at the causes of agoraphobia. When we know something of these we shall be in a better position to see the way forward to a cure.

3.

PRECIPITATING CAUSES

It has been found that many people suffering from agoraphobia can trace the beginning of their trouble to some embarrassing incident, or situation of severe stress, which affected them to such a calamitous extent that they became unduly terrified of the same thing happening again. We say that the incident caused them to be 'sensitized'.

One woman patient, for example, suddenly experienced a violent attack of vertigo (dizziness) at a London theatre. The experience was so devastating to her that she *dreaded* the possibility of it recurring. Afterwards, if ever she went to the theatre, she made sure beforehand that she could obtain a seat by the aisle. Before long she gave up going to places of entertainment altogether, and eventually could not face going out at all. She became a prisoner in her own home, held there by fear.

Another patient, whose case is related by Dr J. A. Hadfield[1], experienced a severe panic one night in the desert during the war. He was going from his office to the officers' mess, as he had done regularly every evening at that same time. But on this occasion the darkness and the solitariness filled him with horror. He was sensitized by it, and for years afterwards he could not cross a park or even a street alone.

[1] Hadfield, Dr J. A. *Psychology and Mental Health*, Allen & Unwin, London.

Traumatic Events

In some cases it is easy to understand the stress and tension which have sensitized the patient. In the case of a woman, for example, the shock of losing a baby at birth, or the emotional and physical strain of a difficult confinement, are very natural causes of severe stress. An unmarried mother may likewise be so caught up in feelings of guilt and the fear of condemnation that she is more easily sensitized, and becomes fearful of going out.

A state of acute shock following a major operation, or a sudden bereavement, may mobilize anxieties that have been latent over many years. Such traumatic events may leave the person wanting in self-confidence, fearful of meeting with other people, and lacking in interest in the world outside. This state of mind provides just the soil in which the seeds of agoraphobia can start to grow, for it tends to establish the habit of remaining at home instead of going out.

Trifling Incidents

Sometimes a really trivial incident will precipitate such a state of panic that it leaves the victim completely baffled. One woman's agoraphobia was triggered off by something which happened on holiday, while she was taking a walk with some friends in the late evening. Her foot slipped as she was going along the tow path by a river, and although she was in no actual danger of falling into the water, the incident left her completely unnerved, in a state of unbelievable panic. From then on she began to go out less and less, until she was unable to leave her home at all.

Another patient dated his fear of going out to an incident in the wartime black-out, when he bumped into a lamp post in the dark. He found his heart pounding at a terrible pace, or so it seemed to him, and he was shocked and terrified to an extent quite out of keeping with the nature of the occurrence.

Bewilderment Adds To the Fear

Such an experience is completely bewildering to the person concerned, and the very fact that it seems so inexplicable only serves to increase the anxiety.

Relatives and friends of agoraphobes need to understand the importance of this. If a person knows *why* he has panicked he can face the issue involved, and is better able to help himself.

put in a non-judgmental way non perjorative
eg describing escalating gain of illness/eg.

He may even be able to avoid such situations in future as far as possible. But if he finds himself caught in such a devastating experience *without any apparent reason*, he is left with no knowledge of what caused it or when it could occur again. This uncertainty greatly increases his anxiety.

Such apparently trifling causes are, of course, more likely to sensitize a person if his nerves are already at a low ebb. But in any case, they betray the existence of deeper fears, which have been mobilized by the incident. We shall look at these more closely in the next chapter.

Prolonged Stress

Sometimes a person becomes sensitized, not by a sudden shock, but as a result of prolonged stress. A long and debilitating illness, for example, can be very wearing, physically and mentally and also emotionally. Negative attitudes take over.

If you have experienced this, you will know what I mean: the tendency to give in to the illness, to retreat from life, rather than take up your responsibilities again. Even the compensations of being ill — the sympathy, friendly visits, gifts of flowers etc. — may be a subtle encouragement to remain housebound in semi-invalidism rather than take up the threads of life once more.

Continued tension of any kind — from frustration, economic worries, harrassment, or just plain overwork (especially where it is not done for one's own satisfaction and pleasure, but in circumstances involving a feeling of injustice and hardship) — leaves the nervous system depleted and renders a person vulnerable: liable to become over-sensitive and caught up in an anxiety state. In such circumstances the least discomfort or extra demand, an unexpected shock, the slightest accident, can give rise to panic.

Obsessive Fear

If the panic is sufficiently great it becomes itself the object of a further fear, as some of you know only too well. 'What is happening to me?', you ask yourself. 'Is this a heart attack? Or am I going mental?' Almost certainly it is neither, but you are so perplexed and worried that you do not know what to think. The whole episode becomes fraught with embarrassment and terror and you are caught in a vicious circle. What started as a sudden experience of panic, or chronic nervous fatigue, now becomes an obsessive fear.

The Threat From Within

As I said in Chapter One, this is not so much the fear of certain external situations, but a *fear of being caught in a panic,* with no supportive help available.

It is this subjective element which distinguishes agoraphobia from many other phobias — the thing one fears is one's own reactions. The street, the bus or train, is not felt to be dangerous in itself. The danger is in oneself, or so it feels. As one patient remarked to me, 'I seem to be at the mercy of something inside myself over which I have no control, and which I do not understand.'

This is just it: if you are afraid, not of something outside yourself but of the panic which is within, you carry the object of your fear within you, and you have no escape from it.

hence sensation of being trapped

Why?

One question will, I know, be in your mind, which I have not yet dealt with. 'Why does it happen?' After all, most people can contain their anxieties; they experience panic only in proportion to the facts of the situation. *Why,* then, do some people react in an exaggerated way, and become permanently handicapped by fears that are quite unjustified?

To find the answer to that question we must look more closely at the factors which influence our emotional development. We shall do that in the next chapter.

4.

WHAT IS THE *REAL* CAUSE?

In the last chapter I discussed the various ways in which a person may become sensitized to a fear of going out. It may be a sudden shock or traumatic experience, or a slow nervous exhaustion which leaves the emotional resources at a low ebb.

But why is it that one person becomes unduly sensitized by an emotional trauma which another person is able to ride successfully? To some extent we are all liable to be thrown off balance emotionally on occasions, but most of us manage to recover our equilibrium in a short time. Why then are some unfortunate people overwhelmed, and increasingly held in the grip of fear? *Is the cause physical or psychological?*

It has generally been assumed that the cause must be psychological, and undoubtedly this is wholly or partly true of most agoraphobes. Recently, however, there is a new theory that in some cases the cause is at least partly a physical one. I refer to the study of organic brain dysfunction (OBD) being carried out at the Institute for Neuro-Physiological Psychology at Chester. The Institute claims that only about 25 per cent of agoraphobes have a *purely* emotional basis for their phobia, and that the remainder have a physical malfunction which aggravates — even causes perhaps — the emotional problem.

Most people, they say, have a little brain dysfunction, i.e. difficulties of functioning caused by small faults within the central nervous system. It can arise from various causes, including a difficult birth and certain types of illness. People who suffer more than a certain amount of brain dysfunction will learn to compensate for it, and often the dysfunction will remain undetected, though some physical and emotional stress will be endured, albeit unconsciously. Sometimes, however, under pressure, the stress becomes too great, i.e. it exceeds the 'tolerance level' and the person succumbs to fear and anxiety. Because he is unaware of his OBD trouble he is all the more frightened of what has happened to him, and so a pattern is started — of panic, and fear of panic. Here could lie one explanation of the fact that some people are sensitized to fear in circumstances which would leave another person almost unaffected.

Opinions vary about the scientific basis for the OBD theory concerning agoraphobia. Do *all* people with more than a certain level of OBD develop agoraphobia? If not, why do *some* suffer in that particular way, and not others? We are brought back to a psychological factor here, surely. But certainly some patients have been helped very considerably by OBD treatment, and any form of help or cure for the phobia should be welcomed.

Emotional Causes

Most of the work being done with agoraphobes is still based on the concept of an emotional rather than a physical cause lying behind the disorder, and even the Chester Institute combines psychotherapy with its remedial exercises. It recognizes that emotional release is very necessary, even if it claims that the emotional problem is caused by the dysfunction.

Let us look then at the emotional problems which can lie behind agoraphobia. I have said that a sudden shock, however slight, may mobilize fears that have been latent for many years. This now requires explanation.

If you are suffering from agoraphobia yourself, you know only too well that your panic is out of all proportion to the situation. The rational part of you — your intellect — is quite aware of this. You have probably tried already to argue yourself out of your fear. You have condemned yourself for 'being so silly'. But it is to no avail: you cannot reason with this fear. It goes deeper than that.

The Right Context

Your fear is illogical in your present-day circumstances. But there *is* a reason for it, and your panic can be understood only when it is seen in its right context — that is, in the light of an earlier emotional experience which was so devastating that it was heavily repressed. It has been 'forcefully forgotten' by the conscious mind, but the memory of it is stored away in the unconscious: it still forms part of your experience.

If anything should happen which has associations with that fear and insecurity of infancy, you experience once again the original feeling of panic, even though you cannot remember the early situation to which it relates. To put it in a more formal way: when the original experience is approximated, the original feelings are reproduced, whether the memory is involved or not.

You can only remember the precipitating cause of your trouble, and you recognize that this does not adequately explain your fear. Your *intense panic* will only make sense when the real meaning of it is discovered.

Relationships

Many writers have noted the importance of the patient's current interpersonal relationships as a factor in the development of agoraphobia. In particular, one psychiatrist in the U.S.[1] has found that his largest category of agoraphobes is that of women who are unhappily married, yet who are not sufficiently self-confident to manage on their own. They feel trapped in the marriage, but cannot face the alternative of having to cope alone, especially if it would mean taking responsibility for children.

It has also been found that such women are often lacking in self-assertion and can become the family doormat — putting up with considerable frustration and suppressing all feelings of anger and resentment.

Their lack of confidence and their propensity for feeling guilty are in fact rooted in the past, and to understand what has gone wrong we need to go back to early infancy, when the foundations of emotional stability are laid.

Identity

The new-born baby is quite unaware of himself as a separate individual, with his own personality and rightful place in the

[1] Wolpe, J. *The Practice of Behaviour Therapy* Pergamon Press, N.Y.

world. Such awareness comes through his relationship with other people, especially his mother. It is through her caring and tenderness that he comes to know he is a person in his own right — wanted, valued, and safe in her acceptance and her love. In such a position of security he can be 'self'-confident, and free to develop his own personality.

Separation Anxiety

Of course, it cannot be said that the baby knows nothing of fear. There are times when he is terribly afraid — of things he does not understand, for instance — but his mother is always there to reassure him. Or is she? The greatest fear the young baby knows is that of separation anxiety or isolation, for he is completely dependent on his mother for a long time, and separation from her spells (to him) disaster, if not actual annihilation. Yet his mother will not *always* be there, and in time the young infant has to learn to tolerate separation from her. He can do this gradually, for longer periods, until he actually comes to the point when he is glad and proud to be independent. He runs away from her — only to peep at her before long to reassure himself that she is still there! But little by little he acquires more confidence to go off on his own; and the more secure the child feels, the better able he is to be independent, and to grow up into a stable and mature adult.

Dependence

What happens, however, if the relationship offered by the mother is poor and unsatisfying? (I am not blaming the mother here: unfortunate circumstances, such as prolonged illness, may create difficulties, and will probably have the same effect on the child as 'poor mothering'.) Does the child reject his 'unsatisfying' mother and cast her off? By no means. Unfortunately the infant cannot turn from her to other resources, for he has none. He is utterly dependent on his mother, no matter how 'unsatisfactory' she may be. She may be angry at his arrival, emotionally inhibited, or quite unable for some other reason to give her baby the warm, intimate, cherishing relationship he needs. But she is his only hope: he has no alternative. The result is that, far from discarding her, he remains frantically clinging to her in his state of insecurity and anxiety. He may even be so overwhelmed that he gives up in despair, and emotionally he returns to the womb.

Regressed Ego

Outwardly, he grows up. He is forced to abandon childhood. His physical and mental growth make that inevitable. But the core of his personality — his ego — is in a regressed state, living a passive existence of absolute dependence.

Here we have the root of the trouble as it has been discovered in many victims of agoraphobia. The personality of such a person is pulled backwards by the frightened and inadequate ego, which is still clinging to the need to be a child, seeking an assurance of love, which is his guarantee of security and protection. This need becomes the more desperate as and when the person experiences greater pressure, tension and anxiety in adult life.

Agoraphobes are defending themselves against deep-rooted feelings of 'un-safety'. And in the unconscious, as a result of the patient's fixation to childhood dependence, safety = home and parents. Here we have the reason for the desire to remain in the safety of the home. Here, too, is a partial explanation of the fact that some such patients can only leave home in the company of another person. It nearly always transpires that the other person represents, in the patient's unconscious, a parent-figure.

Further Insights

Freud, in the course of his psychoanalytic investigations, discovered other more specific factors which sometimes lie behind agoraphobia. These relate to conflicts going on in the unconscious, about matters which have been deeply repressed since early childhood.

You must remember that the fears and anxieties of infancy are particularly terrifying. The young baby feels his hold on life to be extremely tenuous, and all too easily he interprets threats and dangers as putting his whole existence in jeopardy. One thing, in particular, he must do at all costs: he must keep in with his parents, especially his mother, whose acceptance of him is vital. Without her, in his state of helpless dependence, he feels his life to be in danger.

Conflict and Guilt

The difficulty is that sooner or later in his young life he finds out that his own instincts are not always in keeping with his mother's ideas! He learns that he has to conform to certain standards of behaviour, in cleanliness and so on, if he is to keep her love and approval.

If parents are understanding and sensible, they can usually manage to win the child's co-operation without imprinting too much fear on his personality. It sometimes happens, however, that they are so anxious for their children to grow up to be good and well-behaved that they are unduly harsh, or even unintentionally cruel. Such undue anxiety can stem from fear of inadequacy on the parents' part. The question of how to cope if the boy or girl should get out of hand may lead them to ensure that the child is 'kept under'. Such parents may continue to exercise a terribly restrictive influence over their children for many years, causing them to suffer all kinds of guilt feelings: guilt about romance and sex, guilt about standing up for themselves (or even about voicing their own wishes), guilt about expressing emotions of any kind, to cite only a few.

The 'Super-ego'

But why is it that this conflict continues into adult life, even after one has married and left the parental home? The fact is that right back in early infancy, when we first come up against the problem of 'keeping in with' our parents, on whom we are so dependent, *part of our own nature* identifies itself with the 'parent authority' — it 'sides with them', so to speak, so that we have our own *inner* 'parent authority' to keep us on the right lines. This part of our nature is what Freud called the 'super-ego' and it continues to exercise a controlling and restricting influence over us throughout our lives.

So the real warfare, in adult life, is not between our parents and ourselves, but between two parts of our own nature, one of which is hungry for satisfaction while the other — the super-ego — opposes it. This may seem strange. We may imagine that when our parents have died, or even live some distance away from us, parental approval is no longer relevant and the super-ego can be dismissed as redundant. Unfortunately it does not work like that. The super-ego became operative at a time when parental approval was felt to be vital to our well-being, and once established it does not adjust itself to our independence in adult life, but remains tied to its archaic function, and influences us accordingly. (Furthermore, we still have our 'authority figures' in adult life, and we project on to these the experience we had with our parents in infancy.)

In a person who is emotionally mature there is no problem. The rational ego exercises its judgement in regard to the influence of the super-ego and is not completely dominated by it. But in cases of ego-weakness, where there is a great deal of insecurity, the super-ego is allowed to have full sway, amounting to a reign of terror in the unconscious. In such a state of turmoil it is small wonder that the nervous sufferer feels exhausted.

Feelings of Guilt

It is found that many agoraphobes feel trapped in situations from which others would break free. And they are trapped not only by ego-weakness and dependence, but by feelings of guilt: guilt at wanting to leave their spouse and/or children, guilt at having sexual desires, guilt at wanting to leave parents, guilt at expressing anger or resentment — any of these may be found to be relevant in a case of agoraphobia. And the guilt is usually traceable to the dominance of the super-ego over an insecure and frightened self.

The Open Street

Why should the open street become significant? Generally it represents, quite unconsciously, an opportunity and a temptation; and the stricter the person's moral standards the greater the conflict and anxiety.

Broad streets especially seem to suggest an opportunity — for self-expression and self-fulfilment, for sexual activities, for escape from a 'trapping' situation at home, for freedom. Yet, for the agoraphobe, freedom often has associations with (a) unconscious guilt and the felt need of a restraining influence and (b) anxiety about being able to manage on one's own. In a word, FREEDOM spells 'PANIC'.

A Few Illustrations

Some of the matters referred to in this chapter are clearly relevant in the case histories which follow:

C. Edward Barker tells of one patient whom he treated:[1] a lady in middle age who was frightened to go out because she was terrified of fainting in the street. She had been brought up in a strict religious home, and had never married. Preliminary

[1] Barker, C. Edward *Nerves and Their Cure,* Allen & Unwin, London.

conversation suggested the problem was a sexual one, though she firmly rejected the idea. However, later she remembered an early incident when she was assaulted — an experience which left her somewhat shocked, but also excited. There were other encounters in later life in which she enjoyed a certain amount of intimacy, but always with feelings of guilt.

Now it seemed that her natural sexual desires would never find fulfilment, and it transpired in the course of therapy that her fear of fainting concealed a wish to do that very thing — in the unconscious hope that someone might take advantage of her again and give her the satisfaction for which she craved, without the guilt feelings which she would experience in a clandestine relationship. Once the conflict was brought to the surface she found release from her fear of fainting, and was able to go out freely again.

Alan Goldstein tells the story[1] of a woman of thirty-four who went to him for treatment. She had been married for twelve years and had three children. Her anxiety about leaving the house alone dated back to the age of nineteen at a time when her mother was dependent upon her for most of her needs. The girl had to serve her mother and was not allowed to go out without taking her into consideration. She had felt guilty about showing any anger or irritation towards her mother (or her husband), but in the course of psychotherapy she described her mother as critical, domineering, and also fearful of competition, so the girl felt guilty if at any time she was having more enjoyment than her mother. Here was the guilt, and therefore the conflict, about going out.

Another case cited also by Goldstein[2] is that of a 26-year-old woman, brought up in a strict Catholic setting. She had always been extremely conscientious and had put others before herself. Believing the use of contraceptives to be wrong, she had borne five children in six years of marriage and bore the brunt of the responsibility for looking after them. Her husband was busy with his business affairs, and expected his wife to attend to the needs of his parents as well — in particular to act as a peacemaker between them. It was on one such occasion

[1] Goldstein, A. J. *Case Conference: Some Aspects of Agoraphobia* Journal of Behaviour Therapy and Experimental Psychiatry, Vol. I, 1970.
[2] Goldstein, A. J. *Op cit.*

when she was in his parents' house, while they were each trying to win her support in a quarrel, and she was caught in the middle, that her first attack of anxiety came. She had no idea what had happened to her, and became fearful of having another such attack — so her agoraphobia started. Here is the 'doormat' personality: the woman was clearly put upon by her husband and his parents, and she was unable to assert herself, but meekly shouldered responsibilities that were not hers, until the stress became so intolerable that she had her first panic attack.

These three examples may be sufficient to show the kind of conflicts that often lie behind agoraphobia. The person feels trapped 'between the devil and the deep blue sea', i.e. between remaining in an unsatisfying relationship and facing the consequences of leaving it. These consequences are twofold: feelings of guilt, and the prospect of living independently. Sometimes the unsatisfactory relationship is a present one, with husband or parents, but sometimes the really significant relationship is a past one which is still influencing present behaviour, even though the person is unaware of it.

5.

AGORAPHOBIA AND CLAUSTROPHOBIA

So many agoraphobics suffer also from symptoms of claustrophobia that it may be helpful if I say something about the link between the two. They appear to be contradictory, but in actual fact they are often found to be reverse sides of the same coin, as in the following cases.

A young man, the only child of a well-meaning but possessive mother who gave him 'smother-love' instead of the real mother love he needed, felt as though his life was being stifled, and it was hardly surprising that in later years he suffered from claustrophobia.

If he ventured into a lift, for instance, he would panic at once and get out at the first opportunity, sweating and trembling like a leaf. Being in such an enclosed space unconsciously mobilized the old fear of 'suffocation' which was a legacy from his childhood.

At the same time, however, he showed symptoms of agoraphobia which were traceable to his state of dependence. He had reached manhood still being looked after by his over-protective mother, and was quite unable to stand on his own feet. If he went out alone he felt unsafe. Unconsciously he was still in need of protection, even though he was also in fear of being smothered by that same protection. What a dilemma! It was only after bringing the cause of his trouble to light and encouraging the growth of his own ego that he was freed from his phobias and helped towards a position of emotional maturity.

Flight

Phobias are, of course, a form of flight, and this is an instinctive reaction to danger. As little children, if we are frightened we run *away from* the danger, *to* safety (mother's protection). All phobic states constitute a flight from danger to a position of safety. The agoraphobe sees the external world as a threat — and hence the flight to the safety of home. The claustrophobe fears any situation in which he feels stifled, and hence his flight to a position of freedom.

We may also note, in passing, that something amounting to an *obsession* concerning the source of safety establishes itself in both cases. I remember the case of a young lady who only felt safe with her fiancé. One day they were involved in a bad accident in the car, while he was driving, but her obsessive need to cling to him for safety remained, quite unshaken by what had happened.

Trapped!

Now one feature of both phobias becomes apparent — the need for a way of escape; flight demands it. The 'don't fence me in' attitude of the claustrophobe is easy to understand. But why does the agoraphobic patient *also* have a fear of being 'trapped'? 'Surely', you may say, 'one should not feel trapped in the outside world!' But this is just what such a patient *does* feel. If he is on a bus or train he feels trapped because he is not free to get off at any one second; if he is in any crowded situation — a busy store, or street, a theatre or football ground — he feels trapped by the people about him.

He feels hemmed in and caught in a position of danger, without any possibility of making an escape back to the safety of home. But why is this fear of being trapped so important? How does it arise in the first place? Again this takes us back to early life, to a very basic factor in our emotional development. For those who are interested to understand this, I will try to explain as simply as I can something of what is involved.

The Schizoid Factor

Let me at once reassure you about the term 'schizoid'. It does *not* mean 'schizophrenic', but refers to the regressed state which I described in the previous chapter.

You will remember that we saw relationship to be of paramount importance in the development of our personalities.

It is now recognized that the key to psychological development lies in the relationship of a person to his environment. In particular, it is from relationship with other *people* that we develop a sense of our own personality.

What happens if the tiny infant cannot get a satisfactory relationship with the people in his world? He grows up with a sense of unreality; he becomes introverted and withdrawn. If good relationships are just not forthcoming and the anxiety becomes too great, then he tries to deny this basic need. Outwardly he adopts an aloof, unemotional attitude, which avoids *feeling* as far as possible. But inwardly his need of a love relationship is desperate.

Such a person finds himself in conflict — hungry for love and close relationship, yet afraid of entering into any such situation. He may even feel that his own hungry need will destroy the love that does come his way.

The first relationship we know as infants is one of *identification* (with mother, of course). It is only later that we make relationships objectively with her and with other people. But to go from one to the other is quite a big step in emotional development. There is a transitional state in which the individual is torn between the urge to become independent and the fear of abandoning the safety of the identification relationship.

Dr Harry S. Guntrip, one of the greatest authorities on the schizoid state relates the dream of an agoraphobic patient,[1] which shows clearly the conflict between the need to be dependent and the need to become *in*dependent.

The patient, an agoraphobic, dreamed of being in prison. A young man gave him a file to cut through the bars, but he said that it was unnecessary as the doors were not locked. Asked why he did not escape, he replied: 'See how dangerous it is out there! How would I be if I found myself out there all alone?' He then became aware of his mother, the jailoress, standing behind him — though she was not holding him. He was free to go if he had so wished.

This man had previously had many dreams of trying to break out of prison, but in this one we clearly see his ambivalence. He wanted to be free — yet he dare not leave the 'safety' of the prison.

[1] Guntrip, H. *Personality Structure and Human Interaction,* Hogarth Press.

Thus the schizoid patient maintains what Dr Guntrip calls an 'in and out' position. He cannot commit himself to close relationships, yet he is equally afraid of becoming independent. He wants to keep both avenues open, so he tries to 'sit on the fence' and maintain a compromise position of non-committal.

Indecision

Here we can see an explanation of the indecision which characterizes phobic patients. The making of any decision symbolizes, unconsciously, the great underlying decision which the patient cannot take, the one concerning his relationships, so vital to his life.

Yet another reason why this character trait is shared by victims of both these phobias lies in the fact that some decisions are not easily reversed. This means, again, a fear of being 'trapped' — of burning one's boats in certain directions, or shutting the door on one alternative. The claustrophobe may feel this as the fear of shutting himself *in* — committing himself to something from which he cannot escape. The agoraphobe may feel it as a fear of shutting himself *out* — of leaving the 'home' position, or *status quo*, without the possibility of returning.

In all these cases it is the *symbolic* significance of decision-making which presents the difficulty to the phobic patient. But in any case the making of decisions requires some degree of independence and maturity, the ability to take the initiative. The person who is suffering from ego-weakness, or who is withdrawn and introverted, is bound to find this difficult.

Isolation Dread

One feature which is common to both agoraphobia and claustrophobia is the fear of isolation. Again, it may seem strange to speak of isolation dread in regard to a phobia about going into the street where there are people about. You may think this is just the opposite of isolation anxiety. Let me explain.

You will recognize, I am sure, from your own experience, that 'isolation' is not the same thing as 'being on your own'. You may feel more truly isolated in a busy street or on a crowded bus, than when you are alone in the familiar surroundings of your own home.

Dr R. D. Laing tells of a patient who felt rejected and insignificant.[1] She could be on her own, as long as there was no sense of isolation or of being ignored. But she felt *most* insecure in a crowded street, because she became very conscious of the crowds passing her by, without noticing her. It brought to the surface her feelings of unreality, and her unsureness about her own identity.

Again we have to look to very early infancy to see the true significance of isolation anxiety. As I have said, we exist only in relationship with the world about us. *Complete* isolation carries the ultimate threat of non-existence, not only because of our utter helplessness to exist by ourselves physically, but also because our personality demands that we exist in relationship. We need people to be aware of us (that is, we need to feel of some significance to other people) if we are to realize our own identity.

This isolation anxiety manifests itself in claustrophobic fears, for if the patient is shut in, he is also shut off from communication. But a similar feeling attaches to being 'imprisoned' or 'trapped' in the depersonalizing atmosphere of a crowded store or street, where one is cut off from the safety of home by the inability to get away quickly.

Unreality

Any situation in which one is cut off from the 'safety of home' can produce isolation dread, and if this anxiety becomes too great the patient may defend himself against the terror by 'negating' himself. He cuts out feeling, and resorts to a state of depersonalization. His contact with the external world emphasizes his needs and his anxiety, so he withdraws himself emotionally from this environment which is felt to be so dangerous. Unfortunately this proves to be no solution, since the feeling of unreality he experiences in so doing only adds to his anxiety.

Dr Guntrip cites the case[2] of a young woman of nineteen who was chronically agoraphobic, but who felt *claustrophobic* whenever she went into a big store. Analytic therapy revealed the connection between the two: she felt so overwhelmed and

---

[1] Dr R. D. Laing *The Divided Self*, Tavistock.
[2] Guntrip, Harry S. *Schizoid Phenomena, Object Relations and the Self*, Hogarth Press, London.

helpless in the crowded shop that her only 'defence' was one of depersonalization and schizoid withdrawal. This involved a terrible feeling of unreality and lack of contact with everything and everybody, and it was this that led eventually to her agoraphobia.

PART II
THE WAY FORWARD

6.

FREEDOM FROM FEAR

In this second part of the book we are going to look at various ways in which agoraphobia may be overcome. Not every patient responds in the same manner to a particular type of approach. The method which has worked wonders for one may do little for another.

I have heard of patients seeking help from the practice of yoga, from osteopathy, from homoeopathy and many other types of health-giving procedures. The results are not at all clear, but certainly individuals have found help from very many different sources and, as long as the practitioners concerned are fully trained and recognized in their own fields, I see no reason for dissuading people from obtaining help where they can find it.

Spiritual Healing
As someone who has religious convictions, naturally I am firmly of the opinion that religious faith is relevant to every part of life, and those who profess such a faith should 'mobilize' it in their fight against fear.

I can testify to the help I received from my own faith in a battle against the fear of the dark, especially of being outside in the dark. I was plagued by this for many years until one day it seemed to me that such fear was inconsistent with my Christian faith. From then on, when I arrived home in the dark I *made* myself stay outside, albeit for only a minute or so, before going indoors. In this way I gradually proved there was nothing to fear. I 'chatted' to God while doing this, asking his help and his forgiveness for my lack of faith; in so doing I found I was not only losing my fear, but coming closer to God. Faith increases with use!

I am not suggesting that my problem was as severe as that which most agoraphobes face; I do suggest, however, that phobics who have religious convictions can and should bring their faith to bear on their particular problems. This can be done in several ways: by prayerful methods of relaxation, by developing a sense of God's nearness when they are physically alone or afraid, and by affirming that *nothing* — not even panic — can separate us from God's love and power.

Some people have been completely cured of agoraphobia by spiritual healing; very recently I heard of two such cases, and I have known of others. In some cases people have received the laying-on-of-hands from someone who has a special gift of imparting healing in that way. Others found help from their own minister or priest. For those who belong to a church, much help and support come also from the prayers of fellow Christians.

I must add, however, that religious faith does not necessarily work a 'miracle' and provide instant cure. A person's religious belief may well be coloured by his upbringing and by his own neurotic tendencies, so the emotional factors which underlie his phobia may likewise have influenced his faith, and so hinder the healing process. Nevertheless, many people have found great help and strength from their faith, even when a 'cure' has not come about.

Different Forms of Treatment

No one source of help can be guaranteed to cure all patients — if it could, books such as this would not be needed! What I do want to say is that agoraphobia can be cured, indeed has been cured, in different ways.

First I want to ask the question: should one try to *erase* the fear, or should one live through it, in order to overcome it? The methods of therapy which will be described in greater detail in succeeding chapters are based on the latter assumption — that the only way to *overcome* fear is to live through it.

There are other forms of treatment, however, which seek to dispel the fear, either by encouraging right thinking, or by the use of drugs. Certainly the promise of curing the trouble without the awful experience of living through one's fear sounds attractive. Let us look at these possibilities briefly.

Auto-suggestion

One school of thought aims at removing fear predominantly by the encouragement of positive thinking. It is largely a matter of auto-suggestion. If you suggest to your mind that you will be afraid, you will suffer accordingly. But if you suggest to yourself that you will not be afraid, you are much more likely to be serene and confident.

I must admit that I support wholeheartedly the encouragement of positive thinking and affirmation. Indeed, without it any form of therapy is likely to fail. But is it sufficient in itself to effect a sound and permanent cure?

Positive thinking may certainly help an agoraphobe to take the first steps outside the house, and to acquire greater confidence in time. But what of the sudden alarm, the unexpected shock, which could so easily re-sensitize him or her? Even if the person has persevered faithfully and successfully with auto-suggestion techniques over a very long period it is by no means certain that he or she will be sufficiently stable to cope with the *unexpected* anxiety without getting into a panic once more.

Acupuncture

I have heard of patients being treated for agoraphobia by the use of acupuncture. Interestingly, however, I have discovered that in China where this ancient therapy originated it is not used to treat phobias, but this may be because resources are limited and only the worst cases of 'mental' illness receive hospital treatment. In any case, drugs are the normal form of treatment administered.

Nevertheless, acupuncture, as long as it is given by a fully-qualified and experienced person, may be worth trying — some have found it helpful — but do exercise care in the choice of acupuncturist.

Shock Therapy

A treatment which is used not infrequently in this country for patients suffering from depression and other emotional problems is Electro-Convulsive Therapy (ECT), popularly known as 'shock treatment'. Opinions of patients differ greatly about the efficacy of this treatment, and their reactions to it vary considerably. It is seldom used for phobias unless the accompanying depression is really severe. I am not going to explain in detail what happens in the course of such treatment, but merely say that a slight electric current is passed through the person's brain (while he is under an anaesthetic) to produce a mild 'fit'. Previous to this, he has received drugs to relax his muscles so that he is not harmed by the treatment. Doctors do not know what really happens under ECT, i.e. why or how it helps, but it does bring relief to some sufferers. One writer[1] refers to an Aberdare man who received this treatment after suffering from agoraphobia for thirty years. His verdict was that the ECT improved his agoraphobia, but later affected his memory and concentration. Moreover, the benefit was not lasting — his symptoms recurred when stress again became great. He advised other people to avoid such therapy if possible.

Hypnotherapy

This is another method of removing fear, and you may think it could be the ideal answer. Some patients have found great help from such treatment. A newsletter from The Open Door Association once told of an elderly woman who had been agoraphobic for more than seven years, who finally managed to join her family in Australia after a three-months' course of hypnotherapy. We do not know, however, whether the improvement was lasting.

It would be wrong for me to give you false hopes and make rash promises about the likelihood of success if you decide to try this method. In the first place, not all people are suitable subjects for hypnosis. Secondly, it is most essential that the hypnotist is properly trained, not only in hypnosis but also in depth psychology, if he is to give effective help which is well-founded.

At one time hypnosis was widely used by psychotherapists, but experience has suggested that therapy is more soundly based when it involves the conscious will of the patient. Results tend to be less permanent when induced by hypnosis. Nevertheless hypnosis can be a valuable adjunct to other forms of therapy, especially in facilitating relaxation. But do be on

[1] Vose, R. H. *Agoraphobia*, Faber, London.

your guard against charlatans who are not fully and properly trained.

Drugs

For many patients the anti-depressant drug is the only form of treatment suggested or received. This is unfortunate, since such drugs have not been shown to be particularly effective in curing the phobia, though they are no doubt helpful as an aid to relaxation, which is an important feature of any form of treatment. But to *depend* on drugs for maintaining emotional stability is, to my mind, only a second-best substitute for real therapy. Moreover there are many disadvantages to this form of treatment. It is possible that the drugs will have to be continued over a long time, or for ever, unless the patient is ready to wean himself from their use. And trying to break away from the drug habit may prove just as painful as the more radical forms of therapy which I will describe.

Again, can one be sure that there will be no harmful side-effects if the drugs are taken over a long time? Is it certain that they will retain their effectiveness, or will the person require stronger drugs as time goes on?

Furthermore, it can be argued that a sense of fear is necessary for our protection, in certain circumstances. Will the drug make the person less alert and alive to real dangers if and when they arise? I am firmly of the opinion that the best way to conquer fear is to face it.

Treatments Combined

In practice, patients quite often avail themselves of more than one kind of treatment, where available, and most phobia clinics use a combination of different forms of therapy, particularly using hypnosis and/or drugs in conjunction with treatment based on behaviour therapy or psychoanalysis, two forms of treatment which we shall now look at in some detail.

7.

BEHAVIOUR THERAPY

Exponents of behaviour therapy techniques take the view that the *cause* of the phobia is unimportant, and they concentrate therefore on removing the disabling symptoms without probing into the deeper personality problems. Behaviourists see phobic reactions as emotional habits which have been learnt. These are faulty, maladjusted habits, inappropriate (in intensity at least) to the current phobic situation. The cure lies therefore in re-conditioning the person to new habits.

This is done by encouraging and enabling the patient to face his fear — at first perhaps in imaginative work, but ultimately in reality — so that he gradually learns that (i) he can survive his fear and (ii) there is nothing in fact to be afraid of.

When We Were Young
This treatment has sound psychological principles behind it, for it uses the very methods by which we naturally overcome our fears as children — by doing the thing we fear, over and over again.

The little girl who shrieks, with a mixture of excitement and fear, when her daddy throws her into the air, will ask him to do it again — and again. She is putting her fears to the test, and finding they are without foundation. In an earlier chapter we recollected that the toddler does the same thing when he is overcoming separation anxiety — leaving his mother, and then running back to her for reassurance before running off on his own again.

inviting pref to psychiatrist as an
expert of B.T. — an approved practice)
not widely by Ws.

BEHAVIOUR THERAPY   53

We master our fears in this way throughout our life. You may have learned to swim, as I did, by pushing off from the bottom of the sea, and making one stroke before putting your toe down again. Then you tried once more, and made two strokes. Gradually you did a few more, until you found that the water really would bear you up, and your fear subsided.

Behaviour therapy works along similar lines. The patient faces up to his fear *in stages*, and tests it out very gradually until it loses its hold over him.

The Habit of Fear

The technique is based on the fact that a phobia of any kind is an emotional reaction which has become an ingrained habit. Indeed, we might go further and say it has become an *automatic response* to a particular situation. Confront the acrophobe with the view from the Post Office tower, and he will react spontaneously with a fit of terror. Put an aerophobe into an aeroplane and, even before it gets off the ground, you will get a response as sure as a reflex action — panic.

So with your agoraphobia. You have become conditioned to a fear of going out. It is now an automatic reaction, and every time you give in to the fear you are strengthening its hold on you. That habit pattern needs to be broken, by one means or another.

The methods followed by behaviourists vary, but figures seem to show that more phobics find help from this general approach than from any other, so we will look at the main features of the techniques commonly employed.

Desensitization

Desensitization treatment is given at various London hospitals and also in some provincial ones. The method may vary a little according to the views and experience of the therapist, but the following description (given by a patient) of the procedure followed by one psychiatrist is typical:

The patient is taken into a room where he is encouraged to relax. The therapist then breaks down the phobic situation into different parts. For example, in the case of agoraphobia these could include: walking down the path, going through the gate, walking to the postbox three houses away, crossing the road to the bus stop, boarding a bus, and so on. Then slowly and carefully he exposes the patient to the fear experienced at each stage. This is first done in imaginative work in the consulting-room. The patient goes through the situation in fantasy, indicating at each point how severe his feeling of panic is. For if he really enters into this imaginatively, even the *thought* of going down the road will arouse panic.

He numbers his reactions from one to ten — ten representing the stage of complete terror. He may say 'three' or 'four' for 'walking down the path' and it may well shoot up to 'eight' or 'nine' for 'going through the gate'.

During another session the therapist instructs the patient in the art of complete relaxation, and helps him to practise it until he can relax very readily.

At succeeding sessions the therapist takes the patient, again *in imagination,* through the different parts of the situation, beginning with the one with the lowest rating of fear — perhaps 'going down the path'. The patient is fearful as he imagines leaving his front door and going down to the gate. But he is encouraged to relax, and as he does so he finds that his fear lessens, dropping from, say, three to two and then to one. When he can fantasize doing that one small thing with little or no fear, the therapist takes him on to the next.

The same process is repeated with the increasingly fearful aspects of the situation. When sufficient mastery of the fear has been established at each step, in imagination, then and only then, the patient is asked to go out and actually face up to the experience which terrified him and for which he sought help.

It sometimes happens, of course, that a patient finds it difficult to enter imaginatively into fantasy work of this kind. He, or she, may be too tense, or have only limited powers of concentration. In such cases some psychiatrists use a drug to help relaxation, and so make the work a little easier.

Effectiveness

The therapists using desensitization claim that about eighty per cent of their patients receive substantial help from this form of treatment, though they do not assert that the cure is perfect. Many patients learn to *tolerate* the experience, rather than to enjoy it. They can, however, find sufficient release from their particular fear to live much more happily.

Agoraphobia, which has always been one of the most stubborn phobias to cure, has been treated quite successfully by this method. In an article in *The Daily Telegraph* colour magazine some years ago a 49-year-old former sales manager described how he had been helped in this way. His previous work had taken him on long and frequent journeys around the country, but then he developed agoraphobia and for ten years was reduced to doing work at home, being quite unable to leave the house.

In his desensitization treatment he was encouraged to imagine he was going out of the gate, then to the end of the road, and so on. He tells how he eventually went outside and began to conquer his fears in actual experience, in the way he had practised in the course of his sessions in the consulting-room. At the time of writing he could drive up to forty miles in the car, and go into the centre of the town where he lived, without panic.

Contextual Therapy

Very similar in its approach is contextual therapy or *in vivo* desensitization. Here the imaginative work in the consulting-room is omitted, and from the beginning the patient ventures into the phobic situation in reality, with the help and guidance of a trained person. Where the therapist is personally able to accompany the patient for purposes of treatment, this is a great help of course, but it means much time on the part of the therapist and is naturally more expensive. Often, therefore, a trained assistant is allotted to go with the patient, on a regular basis, to help him/her face the fear encountered. This assistant will work closely with the therapist and also attend any groups to which the patient might go for discussion.

Relaxation training often forms an integral part of the therapy: indeed some therapists see it as vital, if the person is to be able to face his fear without undue distress and consequent abandonment of the treatment. Important, too, is the fact that the patient is not pushed beyond what he/she feels ready to face, but is only asked to accomplish what can be tolerated with reasonable comfort on each occasion.

Flooding

By way of contrast, a more controversial form of treatment (known as flooding) consists of pushing the patient into the very situation he fears — under supervision of course — and letting him 'sweat it out' until he gradually discovers that there is nothing to be afraid of. This form of treatment is used much more rarely than *gradual* exposure to the feared situation, and greater care needs to be taken to ensure that the patient is not forced to bear more than he is able to stand.

Group Therapy

Not everyone takes kindly to meeting in groups, and those who are most seriously handicapped cannot easily get to such meetings until some other therapy has already taken place. But for those who can manage it and find groups helpful, they offer a much less expensive way of finding help than one-to-one therapy. There is more hope of finding such treatment within the framework of the National Health Service, than in the case of individual treatment. Some clinics concentrate almost entirely on group therapy; others find it helpful to use it in conjunction with techniques such as those described above. These usually involve not only the phobics but also their spouses, assistants or other friends who are helping the patient. In some groups it has been found that members have been able to help one another — a person with one particular restriction may support another whose trouble is somewhat different.

Other Aspects of Behaviour

Sometimes desensitization is not used at all: the therapist concentrates first on other aspects of the person's behaviour pattern, rather than on the phobic problem. This has been found to work well in cases similar to those cited in Chapter Four, where women patients were found to be lacking in ability to assert themselves. The therapist may feel in such a case that the patient is 'trapped' by her own lack of self-assertion and that an adjustment in this direction will relieve the agoraphobia. Indeed it has sometimes happened that when a person has reached the point of suddenly daring to be assertive, the agoraphobia has disappeared as if by magic! It has to be said, however, that some such cases have been cited relatively soon after the release came, and the long-term results have not been made clear.

Permanent Cure?

The question arises: is the improvement lasting? The answer to this varies enormously. There is evidence that some patients experience no further improvement once the treatment is finished, and that while the situations covered in the course of the treatment can be handled with comparative ease, new situations may provoke just as much panic as previously. In some cases the improvement actually diminishes in time.

Nevertheless, behaviour therapy is the form of treatment most commonly used for agoraphobia, and stands highest in the list of those which patients have found helpful. It is practised widely and it should not be *too* difficult to obtain this sort of therapy unless you live in a somewhat remote area. It also offers scope for self-help programmes — more of this in a later chapter.

8.

IS IT NECESSARY TO
FIND THE CAUSE?

Some behaviour therapists say that finding a childhood cause
of agoraphobia does not help at all in the matter of its cure,
and since the process of psychoanalysis is lengthy and therefore
expensive, there is no point in pursuing that course.

It is quite true that *merely to expose* the cause will produce
only limited benefit. Analysis may be interesting, but only in
rare cases will that alone bring release. It can and does happen
in odd instances, but normally analysis must be accompanied
by a positive therapy involving re-education of the emotions
if the person is to receive the maximum benefit.

However, even Dr Claire Weekes, who has apparently considerable success with her methods of treatment and writes
somewhat disparagingly of analytic techniques, admits that
patients who have improved considerably by desensitization
may, years later, have recurrences of the panic and need to
repeat the treatment in order to desensitize themselves once
more.

Some behaviour therapists do advocate the use of
psychotherapy as well. The Temple University School of
Medicine in the U.S., for instance, describes its treatment of
agoraphobia as two-phased: first the person must learn to deal
with the symptoms of panic, and this is best done in the
situations which each person fears (behaviour therapy used
here). Second, and equally important they say, is psychotherapy — either in group, family or individual format;

addresses issue of
symptom substitution in
lay terms

IS IT NECESSARY TO FIND THE CAUSE?   59

this is necessary because 'interpersonal stresses and conflicts often precede and accompany agoraphobia, and complete recovery depends upon the identification and resolution of these stresses, which are unique to each individual.'

The extent to which such psychotherapy is analytic may vary, but the point is that unless you trace the cause of the panic completely you have not uncovered the *true* nature of the person's problem. We have seen that the panic is out of all proportion to the facts of the present phobic situation and can be explained only in the context of the original emotional trauma from which it sprang. This trauma is still carried in the unconscious, and the true nature of the fear lies hidden and distorted by the forces of repression. It follows that the *emotional need associated with the fear* will not be revealed by desensitization techniques.

What Is Meant by Cure?

The question must be asked: 'What is the patient seeking? What does he, or she, mean by "being cured"?'

Take the case of the lady mentioned in Chapter Four, who was afraid of fainting in the street. It was found that her fear was traceable to inhibitions and conflict concerning her natural need of a close, intimate relationship. Suppose she managed, by desensitization treatment, to overcome her fear of fainting in the street — could it be said that she was cured? Admittedly, she would know great release, and those who treated her *would* pronounce her cured. They would have dealt with the presenting symptom — agoraphobia — but *not* with the needs of her personality.

The behaviour therapists describe phobic reactions as habits which have been wrongly learned; they do not tell us why that came to be so. We are told that the cause of the trouble is irrelevant; the thing to do is to cure it. Now the point is that when the real cause of the trouble is found — when we see *why* the habit of panic has established itself — we come upon the *deeper* need of the person, and can deal with that accordingly. It is a question of whether one wants to cure a symptom, or heal a personality.

In the case of this lady, the desperate frustration would still be there and would probably find some other outlet, just as depressing. How much more fulfilling her life will be if the underlying inhibitions are brought to the surface and dealt with.

The agoraphobia will in any case lose its force when once the cause of it has been exposed. The patient can then more easily be re-conditioned to the habit of going out instead of staying in.

If the agoraphobe is seeking only to overcome his fear of going out, then behaviour therapy may work wonders, and enable him to live a much happier life. But such treatment does not get down to the basic problem of understanding and meeting the needs of, for example, the tiny immature ego, still clinging inwardly to dependence on mother. Analytic psychotherapy uncovers this, the real need, and seeks to meet it.

Wholeness

Those who say that agoraphobes can be cured by desensitization alone, judge from the results in terms of the ability to go out. Psychotherapists are concerned with the wholeness of the personality. Without the use of analytic techniques the underlying cause of the phobia — the conflict or ego-weakness — is not recognized; neither is the basic emotional need of the patient met.

It may be argued, of course, that when the fear of going out is dealt with, there is a great deal of improvement in self-confidence and stability of the personality generally. This is true. The ability to live a normal life once more, the freedom from fear, and from feelings of guilt and failure — these, and many other factors, help a great deal towards re-integration of the personality.

I feel bound to say again, however, that dealing with the fear of panic without looking for the root cause of the terror does not resolve the intra-psychic conflict, nor does it meet the deep, emotional needs of the person which have not in any case been brought to the surface.

One cannot know the true extent of a person's need, merely by combating the fear. As someone has said: 'It's like trying to cure measles by treating the spots.' It is treating a symptom, while the illness remains. It is liable to break out in some other form, but in any case it is debilitating.

My own attitude, therefore, would be not *merely* to cure the fear of panic and so enable the patient to go about more freely, but to help him to *go forward to wholeness*. Perhaps, as a practising psychotherapist, I am biased in my views — but then I have had, in the course of my training, a full training analysis. No one could therefore convince me that analytic psychotherapy has little to offer. My own experience is quite undeniable.

Investment in Happiness

It is true, however, that this form of treatment is lengthy and also expensive. It must be regarded, in fact, as an investment: an investment in future happiness and fulfilment, in emotional stability and in freedom, not just from the fear which is a *symptom* of intra-psychic 'dis-ease', but from the disease itself.

When that is achieved, then as one patient recently remarked in my hearing: 'It is like being born again, almost literally. I am a new person.'

Yet it need not be a case of either . . . or. Both techniques have a place in helping patients. Analytic psychotherapy need not preclude the practising of behavioural techniques. Indeed, in some cases these are necessary if the patient is to get to the therapist at all. But the analytic therapist will not be content to enable the patient to go out. He will meet the greater challenge: of helping him, or her, to become emancipated from the underlying conflicts, inhibition, and state of dependence which otherwise will continue to exercise a backward pull on the personality, and rob the person of a great deal of happiness and fulfilment.

In a word, he aims for 'wholeness'.

9.

ANALYTIC PSYCHOTHERAPY

Bearing in mind the deeper causes of phobias (see Chapters Four and Five), some patients prefer to get down to the original root of the trouble by means of analytic psychotherapy. This may be done in group sessions or individually, but I will confine myself to a description of 'one-to-one' analysis.

The analyst may ask you to relax on a couch, though this is not a universal practice: some therapists these days prefer to talk to their patients in the more normal setting of easy chairs.

Again with this form of treatment it is necessary for you to face your fear. Your therapist will help you to relax and talk freely to him about the situations you fear most, and he will enable you to see the basic constituents in your anxieties. You will probably discuss your present situation and your relationships with others at home and at work. No doubt you will also discuss the precipitating factor which triggered off your first terrible panic, and the background of events at that time.

Dreams
Don't be surprised if your therapist asks you to tell him your dreams, for if there are serious conflicts going on in the unconscious they will probably come to the surface *in a disguised form* in your dreams. Elements of ego-weakness and insecurity will likewise be revealed. From his expert knowledge and training the therapist will see through the disguise and help

you to recognize the emotional difficulties that are troubling you, and which normally you do not allow to come to the surface. You will find these have a bearing on your phobia.

'Association'

Apart from this, you will probably find yourself engaging in what is known as 'association' — this may be directed by the therapist, or at other times it will be 'free association' which means you allow your mind to 'free-wheel' and think aloud, sharing your thoughts and feelings with your therapist. Such thinking inevitably gravitates to the conflicts that are there below the surface. I say 'inevitably' — and that is true, as long as the association really is free and uninhibited.

The trouble is that pain, fear, embarrassment or guilt can act as a resistance against letting your thoughts and feelings go just where they will. Unconsciously you will tend to put the brake on them, or 'edit' them, and the therapist has to recognize what is happening and help you over the difficulty.

You will also meet with this factor of resistance when you try to recapture the painful experiences and feelings of childhood, where the root of your trouble lies. Again the therapist will make you aware of this resistance, and give you his reassurance and help so that you can overcome your fears. (There are other aspects of resistance, which are dealt with in Chapter Eleven.)

The Original Anxiety

As the analytic work proceeds, you will discover the reason why your panic is so exaggerated: it does not belong to your present-day experience at all. It is being 'projected' on to these situations, but really it refers to anxiety felt in your earliest years.

In the course of your therapy you will be encouraged to go back into those feelings, in imagination. This is not the same sort of imaginative work as that used in desensitization, for here you are going back in fantasy to the original experience, which aroused such panic that you probably thought you were being annihilated.

In the early situation it was a matter of life and death, or so it felt to you at the time. Tiny infants cannot see beyond their anxiety. They cannot look ahead and know that the danger will pass. The present moment is eternity. They have no means of knowing that their fears are exaggerated. They can use no powers of reason to help themselves.

The whole life of an infant in its early months consists of feeling. Security is life; anxiety is death. No wonder your panic is so great, when it relates, in fact, to the time when you actually thought this was the end.

It is also true that an infant's emotions, when experienced very strongly, are felt to be dangerous *in themselves*. It is as though the baby fears being overwhelmed and destroyed by the very force of emotions which he cannot control. This is another source of the very real panic felt by agoraphobics.

Such early emotions and anxieties can be brought back to consciousness with the help of a trained therapist. This is the analytic part of the therapy. What of the cure? Does the trouble disappear when you discover its true cause?

It is possible, of course, that the agoraphobia will be much relieved, or disappear altogether, when the patient sees that it is a spurious fear: when the true significance of the fear is brought to light and seen for what it is. It usually takes some further work, however, before the trouble is cured.

Therapy
It is obvious that what has to be done now is to deal with the *true* anxiety which has been brought to the surface. For instance, if the anxiety is connected with guilt, then the guilt complex has to be dealt with. If it comes from a fear of isolation, then the therapy is directed towards this.

You may wonder how a therapist can free you from your complexes, inhibitions and conflicts. How does the *therapy* work? It is difficult to give a straightforward, simple answer to this question, in view of the many differing needs of patients, each of whom has his own particular background, his own individual problems, and his own response to different forms of therapy; and therapists work in many different ways.

In general it may be said that two features are common. Firstly, the therapist offers a consistent, supportive and accepting relationship to the patient, in the face of whatever the patient has to tell him. Whatever aggression, or guilt, immature dependence or other traits of character come to the surface, the therapist accepts the patient as he is, giving him a reassurance that he is safe and secure.

The importance of this relationship cannot be over-emphasized. Remember that the fear goes back to babyhood, and in the life of a tiny, dependent baby, relationship is paramount. It is the one source of security — *or* of insecurity and anxiety.

Secondly, the trained psychotherapist can also explain, or interpret, the patient's feelings and demonstrate how they came to be experienced, and why they caused such intense anxiety. This makes it possible for the patient to replace the negative emotions with the positive motivations which make for wholeness.

For example, if a woman suffering from agoraphobia is found, during analysis, to be the victim of sexual inhibitions, the therapist can, as the trouble comes to light, explain the deep roots of her inhibitions, and so help her to a positive and healthy view of intimacy and romance. He thus helps to free her *not only* from her agoraphobia, *but also* from the inhibitions which have greatly impoverished her life. She is enabled to go about more freely but, more than that, she can find fulfilment in richer, more satisfying relationships, because of settled conflicts.

You can see what psychotherapy aims to do. It not only makes you face up to your present fear, but it encourages you to see the deeper meaning behind it, so that emotional conflicts and weaknesses of long-standing are brought into the light of day and dealt with. This goes to the heart of the trouble, to the point from which any radical cure must begin.

10.

METHODS OF SELF-HELP

Inevitably there are very many agoraphobic patients who, by reason of their emotional condition, just cannot get to a hospital or therapist. If they are to find relief at all, it must be by some method which enables them to help themselves. Fortunately there are several ways of doing this.

Desensitization

This method does lend itself to self-help reasonably well, though naturally it is more difficult on your own than with the help and encouragement of a therapist. But Dr Claire Weekes, a consultant physician in Australia, has done a great deal of work with patients who are unable to get to a therapist, and claims considerable success. She has produced books, records and cassettes which can be purchased by agoraphobes to give them the guidance and help they need, and many testify to the progress they have made by following her suggestions. In particular this form of help is invaluable for those who are afraid, or unable, to go to a trained person for treatment.

Four Principles

Dr Weekes describes her method as having four basic principles.[1] She calls them: (1) facing (2) accepting (3) floating

[1] Weekes, Dr Claire, *Peace from Nervous Suffering*, Angus & Robertson, London.

and (4) letting time pass. Her advice is:

1. *Do not try to force yourself to forget your fear — face up to it, acknowledge its existence.* Now this is surely sound advice, for you will never solve a problem if you are trying to forget it exists.
2. *Do not fight against the fear, but accept it.* In this way you will not perpetuate and aggravate things by piling on what Dr Weekes calls 'second fear', that is, the 'What if . . .' and 'Supposing . . .'
3. *Do not tense yourself against the fear, which will only increase stress, but rather let it have its way for the time being.* Go with the feeling; let it pass through you, as it were, until it has spent itself.
4. *Do not be discouraged because you are not cured in a few days, or even weeks.* Do not spend too much time in introspection and disappointment at your failures. Be prepared for the process to take time.

This last point is important. Many patients are far too hard on themselves. They forget that the wrong emotional habits have been going on over a long time, and cannot be wiped out straight away. Do not set a time limit on your recovery, and give up if you don't make it. Be patient with yourself, and let time pass without worrying over it: or you will be re-sensitizing yourself to worry all over again!

The Step-by-Step Approach

So much for the basic principles. What are you to do to help yourself in practice, in this desensitization process? Follow, if you like, the technique I have described in Chapter Seven, as far as you can. You will need to give yourself several sessions of, say, half-an-hour each on some of the stages.

1. Practice the art of relaxation. There are many books to help you, or you may follow the following technique: lie on a comfortable bed and let all your muscles become completely loose. Be aware of this relaxation in every part of your body. For example, concentrate on your toes, ankles, knees, thighs and hips. Then on your shoulders, arms, wrists, fingers and thumbs. Finally your back, tummy, chest, nape of the neck, jaw, facial muscles and brow. Feel

that *every* part of you is relaxed.

2. When you are completely relaxed physically, allow yourself to relax mentally. Let all thoughts of duties and responsibilities go. Let all worries go: *at this moment* you have nothing to worry about. You are safe and secure. A little auto-suggestion will probably help you here. Affirm quietly to yourself that with every breath you take you are becoming more relaxed. As you breathe in more deeply, you are becoming more deeply relaxed. Practise this art of relaxation until you have really mastered it.

3. Now face up to the fears of the situation which frightens you, by breaking it down into parts, as suggested in Chapter Seven, and feeling the *severity* of the fear at each point.

4. Now you are ready to imagine the situation which you fear, recognizing the fear and letting it have its way, yet relaxing in the knowledge that you are safe. *Fear cannot harm you*, so don't be afraid of feeling it. Follow the method I have described in the previous chapter. As you imagine, say, walking down the path to the gate, *let the feeling of fear come;* but *relax at the same time* in the way you have practised, until you feel the fear gradually subsiding.

5. When you have mastered the fear in the *least* frightening part of the situation you can go on to deal with the more difficult aspects of it. It is important for you to go right through the situation in detail, even to the most terrifying incidents that could happen.

Face the Worst, in Imagination
Are you imagining going for a bus ride? Then go through all the trifling things which might unnerve you. See yourself being jostled as you get on. Hear the conductor's voice saying 'Pass along the bus, please' — the last thing you want to do! Imagine, if you like, the glare of the woman next to you, as she bundles all her big parcels on to her lap to give you a seat. Perhaps you find you have only a note for a small fare. The conductor glowers at you and murmurs something under his breath. Use your imagination to go through all the possible emergencies you can think of — the things which you, personally, would

find unnerving. Maybe, for example, you see the bus still crowded as you reach your destination, and you have to squeeze past several standing passengers to get to the door.

In fantasy, go through the worst that could possibly happen, and face up to the fear at each point. But remember that as you feel the panic *you also allow yourself to relax*, and you will become aware that the panic is actually falling away from you.

Relaxation Is All-important

A great deal of the success of this form of therapy depends on the element of relaxation. This is why some psychiatrists use drugs to help patients who are very tense.

So many patients say: 'I just *can't* relax'. I expect you have read articles and booklets on the art of relaxation. I wonder if you have *seriously* tried to follow the suggestions contained in them, whether you have really *persevered* with the techniques and exercises recommended. It is so easy to make a half-hearted attempt, and then give up. I know it is difficult, if you have been living on your strain and stress, to believe that anything else is possible for you. But a lot is at stake, so do be encouraged to persevere.

Now For the Reality

When you have mastered your fear imaginatively from the safety of your room, you are ready to do the same thing in the real world outside. If you have been quite unable to leave the house at all, go from your back door to the dustbin. If you feel the panic starting, don't rush back to the house, but *relax* until the fear gradually falls away from you.

Repeat that same little experiment until you can do it with very little fear; then try to go a little further — cross the path to the garage. When that ceases to terrify you, try to go as far as the gate; later you can go outside the gate and along to the postbox a few yards away. Continue in this way until you can get to the bus-stop and board a bus for a short journey.

(Of course, despite my suggestions for imaginative work, you should actually make things as easy as you can for yourself the first time — choose a time when the bus will not be crowded, and see that you have some small change for the fare.)

I can imagine you saying that you doubt very much whether you can really do this. It sounds too difficult. Remember that others have felt as you do, but have had the courage to try,

and have found considerable release by following this method.
You can do the same — if you really want to.

That last phrase is important, and is not so harsh and
unfeeling as it sounds. I will explain more to you about this
in Chapter Eleven.

Persevere Despite the Fear

Of course it will not be easy. If you give up as soon as you panic,
you will be back in your prison again. It is only by facing the
fear, and living through it, realizing that the *fear itself cannot
harm you,* that you will gradually lose your anxiety and find
freedom.

Do not wait until you think you can go down the road
without fear, or you may wait for ever. The important thing
to remember is that you can do it *despite the fear* you may feel.
So make a start *now.* If you have already faced the fear, in your
fantasy, and felt it subside, when you step out into the garden
or the street you can expect your panic to be less than it has
been. But don't expect to be *completely* fearless when you
go out, or you will quickly be disappointed and give up. Your
fear can and will subside if you allow it to. (You have already
learned this in your imaginative work in your room.)

It is a case of experiencing the fear again and again, accepting
it rather than letting it upset you, until you become almost
impervious to it. It will cease to bother you, and become
irrelevant. It has been said that there is no worry so small but
it will grow if you feed it with attention. The same is true of
fear, and this is what has been happening to you. You have
worried about your fear. You have fed it with attention. Fear
can be 'starved to death' if one accepts the fact that it is there,
and then goes on living in spite of it. As I said this takes some
courage and determination. Yet this is the way forward.

Is There an Easier Way?

You may well feel that the desensitization method I have
described involves too much discipline, too much
concentrated and consistent effort, for you to be able to manage
on your own, and perhaps you cannot leave the house to go
to a trained therapist.

'Is there a simpler solution?' you ask. I do appreciate how
you feel, especially if your problem is not merely a specific
limitation, but one of general nervous tension which seems

to bar you from concentrating on imaginative work.

Let us be realistic. Desensitization involves exposing yourself to fear, in order to master it. It has something in common with the medical technique of immunization, in which you take a small dose of the illness in order to build up your power to withstand its onslaught and overcome it. You do have one choice, however, in the present case. Either you expose yourself to the fear gradually, by a planned recovery method, or you take the bull by the horns and see what happens.

Taking the Plunge

There *are* people who have had the courage to do their own form of 'flooding' — jumping in at the deep end, with only a little preparation — and have found it works. One article in a Sunday newspaper told of a 62-year-old widow — we will call her Mrs A. — who had been a prisoner in her own home for eleven years. To step outside the door put her in a terrible panic. Neighbours collected her pension and did her shopping for her. Meanwhile she spent her leisure hours doing jig-saw puzzles, watching television and listening to records.

She had been a foster-mother for many years, and a former foster-child, now married and living thirty-four miles away, had often invited her to stay. But it was quite impossible for her to contemplate making the journey — or so it seemed. One more invitation came and Mrs A. decided to make, as she put it, a 'once-for-all effort'.

The travelling was arranged to make it as easy as possible for her. A friend and his family took her in their van. She managed the journey reasonably well, with the children to occupy her attention. Then one day, while she was away, her hostess said: 'Put your coat on — we're going shopping.' After spending some time in the shops, they went into a restaurant for a meal. Further outings followed, during her short stay of six days, and the fact that someone was with her helped to make it easier. But the real test came when she went home — *alone*, by bus. Mrs A writes: 'We came up the M1 — the first time I had seen a motorway. The day was dull and the scenery ordinary but I began to enjoy it — seeing the trees and fields, and realizing that *my fear was fading*. Only when I got home did it begin to sink in that I had beaten the fear. I cannot describe how dreadful it has been. Just to step outside the door put me in a terrible panic. Now it is almost like being born again. I can go out *without a qualm*, catch buses and do my own shopping.'

A Struggle

It is only fair to say, however, that not everyone who has tried
this way has found it so easy. Mrs B., writing in a weekly paper,
makes it clear that for her it has been and still is, a struggle all
the way.

Her agoraphobia followed a period of physical illness and
nervous breakdown. She decided she must fight against the
phobia if she were to regain any sort of normal life, and it
seemed easier for her to venture out when it was dark and the
street was deserted. With the help and encouragement of a very
understanding husband, she took the plunge at ten o'clock one
night. She went one hundred yards down the road, and came
back sobbing. She did not force herself to do this every night,
but as often as she could she braved the night air, gradually
covering greater distances.

That was nine years ago, and she continued to 'persevere
despite the fear' — a good motto for agoraphobics! It has been
uphill all the way for Mrs B. But she did improve sufficiently
for her to take her daughter to school, and do her own
shopping. She could go back to the church to which she
belonged, and just occasionally she could manage a visit to a
restaurant or a theatre.

Her article makes it plain, however, that the battle still rages;
she says she has learned to live a tightrope existence. She is
still unable to travel on buses or trains, and there is a constant
strain whenever she goes out. She suffers still from rising panic
and claustrophobia in public meetings of any kind, and if a
minor illness keeps her indoors for a day or so, the resultant
setback is hard to bear.

Obviously this is not a cure. This courageous lady has learned
to live with agoraphobia, and none but her close friends realize
her difficulties. She has, by her determination, made life a little
easier for her family as well as for herself, but it is not the perfect
answer.

Perhaps one clue to Mrs B's difficulty lies in her own phrase
'I knew I had to *fight*'. In actual fact, the important thing about
any attempt at desensitization is to learn to *relax*. As I have said,
this is one of the main points about doing imaginative work
before you venture out into the street. By learning to relax in
your fantasy work at home, you will more easily apply the same

technique when you go outside to put it into practice.

You may wonder why Mrs B. found it so difficult, while Mrs A. seems to have found 'instant release'. Why does it work for one and not for another? The answer to this probably lies in the different temperaments and backgrounds of the two people. As I said earlier, no two people respond to the same form of therapy in exactly the same way. You must also remember that Mrs B. had to contend with the after-effects of a *general* physical and nervous breakdown (including, incidentally, a period of depression following a miscarriage while she was fighting her agoraphobia).

Planned Recovery

Perhaps you have tried taking the plunge, with such 'disastrous' results, in terms of panic and upset, that you dare not try again. Yet you may also feel that the imaginative preparation I described in the previous chapter is beyond you. Then try a simpler form of planned recovery.

If you have just one friend who will help you, so much the better, especially if you live alone. It can be very wearying and disheartening to go battling on, with no one to share your minor victories and give you encouragement when you might be tempted to give up. It is also true that trying to go out for a short walk 'just for the sake of it' can seem very pointless. A friend may help to make your short 'outings' more purposeful.

If she lives close at hand you may get to the point of making a daily visit to her house for coffee, or for tea. You will no doubt find some way of repaying her kindness as you are able. Don't be too embarrassed or independent to accept such help; I am sure your friend will be just as thrilled as you are about your progress, and she will get great satisfaction from having had a hand in your recovery.

Perhaps your only contact can be by way of letter or telephone, but it will still mean quite a lot to you to be able to share your ups and downs with someone else. If you do live alone, it may also be a good idea to keep a diary. If you cannot report on your progress to another person, at least you can record it here. It will enable you to look back after a while, too, and see how far you have come. But remember what I said earlier in this chapter about not setting your sights *too* high, or putting a time limit on your recovery. Don't be dismayed by setbacks, but accept them as being only temporary. You can and will recover from them if you are patient with yourself.

No one is in a position to *promise* a complete cure to any patient, where emotional troubles are concerned, and agoraphobia is no exception. Some patients improve, but continue to find life a struggle at times. Others, whose release is more complete, become so overjoyed that they take a delight in going out as much as possible. Such a person may become quite a globe-trotter, making up for lost time!

So much depends on the patient's personality, early life and upbringing, environmental stresses, and the deep underlying cause of the phobia. Nevertheless, be on your guard against making this an excuse to remain in your unhappy state. You may have been 'imprisoned' in your home for many years, but you do not have to make it a 'life sentence'. Let the experience of others encourage you. It shows you what can be done, and it is good for you to accept the challenge that it presents to you.

Tracing the Trouble to its Source
It is difficult to engage in self-analysis, if only because of the factor of 'resistance', of which something has been said already, but which will be dealt with more fully in the next chapter. Yet you may want to trace your trouble to its source, and be unable to find an analytic therapist in your area; in any case such treatment is expensive. Here, then, are some suggestions as to how you may help yourself to gain deeper insight into your own particular problem.

1. Keep a private notebook and jot down the situations which make you fearful, noting especially what they have in common, and the *exact feelings* you experience.

2. Write down in detail, as clearly as you can remember it, the precipitating cause of your fear — the incident which sparked it off. Do this as soon as you can, before some of the details are lost.

3. Make a careful note, too, of the background of events at the time or immediately prior to the incident, which may prove significant (as in the case I describe below). Especially include in this anything which may have disturbed your equanimity in any way at all — a disagreement, disappointment, a criticism or injustice, embarrassment or conflict.

4. If your phobia was not triggered suddenly but came on gradually after a period of illness or difficulty of some sort, write down as much as you can recollect of your feelings at the time. Was there any sense of failure, or guilt, of inferiority or injustice, for example?

5. Practise the art of relaxation. Do this regularly and take it seriously, using the suggestions earlier in this chapter, or any book on relaxation which you find helpful. You do need to be relaxed, physically and mentally, if you are to allow your *feelings* to come to the surface.

6. Now you are ready to do some 'association'. First relax yourself, and then take yourself, in imagination, to some situation which fills *you* with terror — say the theatre, or a supermarket. Let your feelings have full rein, and see where they take you in memory or imagination. Where and when have you felt like this before? If you trace it back far enough you will, I'm sure, find yourself back in childhood or early infancy.

7. What is the basic element in your fear? Are you, for instance, afraid of authority, or of the intensity of your emotions, or of being lost and forgotten? Are you afraid of being rejected and not wanted? Try to pin down the feeling if you can, and follow it as far as possible.

8. 'Associate' in this same way, with regard to the precipitating cause and its background as you have noted them (in 2. and 3., or 4.). Where does this take you, if you let your feelings carry you back? Remember it is the *feeling* which has the association with the past, so concentrate on that as much as possible.

9. As you do this, you will probably begin to trace some history of your feelings back towards the original trauma which has *really* caused the trouble. It is unlikely that you will get to this in the course of just two or three attempts, but if you persevere, when you are able to get some time to relax, I am sure you will find some insights coming to you.

An Illustration

Let me give you an example which will illustrate some of the points I have mentioned. They concern the case of the army major, related by Dr Hadfield, to which I referred on page 26.

You may remember his agoraphobia was precipitated one evening as he was crossing the camp to the officers' mess, in the Egyptian desert. He felt an awful dread of the darkness, the space and the solitariness. Associating to this, he recollected an episode at the age of six when he ran away from home one night, and found himself in an open field, filled with terror in the darkness. His self-will in running away had taken him into danger, and he returned home much chastened and became obedient and docile.

Some relief of his phobia followed when this memory came back, but his trouble was not cured. His associations took him further back, to an incident when, after a bout of naughtiness on his part, his rather cruel nurse took him by the throat and he felt his life to be in danger. It happened on the open sea-front, where no help was in sight, and he had no alternative but to submit. Again, in this earlier incident, his self-assertion had run him into danger.

The open space of the desert, the darkness and the solitariness had obvious associations with the past, but this was still not the final answer. Why did the major have a fit of panic on that *particular* evening? He had, after all, crossed the camp in the same way, and at the same time, night after night.

Further inquiry revealed that prior to the incident on the night in question, there had been an argument with a fellow officer. The major knew he was in the right and wanted to assert himself, yet he feared the row involved. There was a further complication, in that if he gave in and did as the other officer wanted, he would find himself faced with a court martial for breaking regulations. He was trapped 'between the devil and the deep blue sea' (a situation which, we noted earlier, is often relevant in the lives of agoraphobics). The major was in an intolerable situation, and it was the *conflict* (should he assert himself, or should he give in?) which really lay behind the phobia, and had associations with his early childhood with its terror of being abandoned. This insight, coupled with some positive therapy aimed at resolving that conflict once and for all, which brought him release.

You can see, here again, the difference between the two types of therapy I have described. The major might have been freed from his agoraphobia by some form of desensitization treatment. But the more radical approach of psychotherapy revealed the *real* trouble. With the therapist's help he was enabled to acquire a new confidence in his own personality, and in his right to assert himself when necessary. His life-long conflict concerning authority, which had been repressed in the unconscious, was resolved.

Re-educating Your Emotions

This brings me to the fact that when you have gained insight into the cause of your problem you must set about re-educating your emotions. Almost certainly you will have discovered that some form of early insecurity lies behind your trouble. Recognize that this was all in the past. Because of your helplessness you were devastated by it at the time. It was felt as a threat to your very survival. But that is over now. You can put it behind you. Your existence is no longer threatened.

Nurture yourself in feelings of inner security. Affirm the validity of your own personality — it is your birthright. Adopt a new attitude towards yourself, in which you respect yourself and your wishes as much as you do those of other people. What we call self-denial, i.e. going without one's own pleasure on occasions for the sake of others, should have a place in all our lives, but it does *not* mean negating our rights and wishes all the time — 'caving in' on every occasion because of a fear of asserting ourselves. You need to have a healthy respect and liking for *yourself*. Feel that it is good to be you!

You will find that when you become more secure as a person, life begins to open up. As you become motivated by positive aims, instead of the need to cope with inner conflicts, inhibitions and anxiety, it will make a *tremendous* difference to your life.

11.

RESISTANCE

It may seem very strange to you when I say that your efforts to break free from your prison of agoraphobia will inevitably meet with resistance. No, not from the family: they will be only too pleased to have you restored to your usual active self. Oddly enough it is *you* who will resist getting better. It is very important that you should recognize this and understand it, because if you are aware of the danger you will be on your guard against it.

It is true to say that every person who suffers from an emotional disorder tends, *unconsciously*, to sabotage his own attempts to put things right. Let me explain this more fully.

One part of you — your rational, intelligent self — is quite determined to find a way through your dilemma, and to enjoy life normally and fully once more. But you must remember that your phobia serves a very real purpose in the unconscious.

Defence

We have seen that your phobia is a *defence against a still deeper fear* — a basic insecurity in one form or another. This insecurity dates from a time when you were *utterly helpless* and quite unable to cope with your terror. It seemed a threat to your very survival. You could not counter it by argument, nor could you look ahead to the time when it would pass. You did the only possible thing, if you were to survive. You repressed the fear, and the cause of it, deeply in your unconscious. The intensity of that panic reasserts itself on occasion today, but you no longer feel *totally* insecure — you have projected the original fear on to the fear of the street, so that you can now deal with it: you can avoid the panic by staying indoors. So this new fear is a *defence — against feeling the even more terrifying fear* you experienced as a child. Such a defence is not going to be given up lightly.

False Security

Unconsciously you even find a certain security in your present position. You have been imprisoned by your fear for a long time. The prison is uninteresting and monotonous and has severe disadvantages perhaps. You long to be free. But the prison also has one advantage: it has a certainty about it. You know where you are in this prison. This is the way of life to which you have adapted yourself — it is familiar ground.

By contrast, the world of freedom offers you adventure, new experiences and new friends. Can you take all this? Can you bear to leave the prison, with its certainty (unsatisfactory though it is) to find your freedom? (Remember the dream of Dr Guntrip's patient, quoted in Chapter Five).

I am not merely talking here in terms of the *house* being your prison where you feel safe — it is something much more fundamental and more subtle than that. I am referring to your emotional 'life-style'. Its very uniformity gives you a 'safe' feeling. (To illustrate this point from other disorders, I could say that the invalid may feel more at home with illness than with good health; the victim of depression is in familiar territory when he is in the throes of despair; the 'martyr' finds satisfaction in his martyrdom — and so on.) The 'safety' is not well-founded, but it feels better than nothing.

Compensations

It is possible that you are finding other compensations, too, from your present situation. It is a fact of human nature that we do find consolation in our distresses, and a good thing we do: it helps us to overcome our disappointments.

A man who loses the chance of a better job with another firm may be comforted by the knowledge that he would have had to move to a district where the housing position could be very difficult. Or you may lose a dress you saw in the shop window a short time ago, and you console yourself with the

medicalisation — patients we only
such in a relationship
ie ī doctor ...

thought that at least you have saved your money!

We adapt ourselves to circumstances in this way, and on the whole is makes for a more positive, contented life. But when our health is at stake (physically, mentally or emotionally) it is a very different matter. For we are in danger of accepting negative satisfactions (illness, anxiety, guilt, etc.) instead of the _real_ wealth of happiness, health and fulfilment.

Your phobia may have brought you sympathy and attention, even significance (which is something every one of us needs). Perhaps your family or friends show a concern for you — more than they did before. It could also be that because of your 'disablement' you manage to escape other duties or responsibilities that you used to find irksome: social visits, looking after elderly in-laws, etc.

Unconscious Motivations

There is no condemnation implied or intended here. You are the one who is suffering; you _want_ consciously to be free. But it is important that you should be alive to the _unconscious motivations_ which will drag you into accepting 'substitute' satisfactions instead of the real thing.

Dependence

Finally a word about another possible source of resistance: your own dependent needs. You may remember that one feature of most agoraphobes is their 'ego-weakness' — their need to cling to the safety of home. This has yet another facet.

Patients who are very dependent have great difficulty in regard to relationships with other people. They hunger for love, yet they fear to trust it when it comes. It _could_ be that an agoraphobic wife is unconsciously trying to keep her partner at home, to reassure her of his love. If there has been any underlying doubt about the other's love, the agoraphobia may be a desperate attempt to divert attention to oneself.

Another result of this difficulty in making relationships is that the patient shies away from social activities and retires into his shell, his own inner world. It is not a satisfactory world, and it has its own anxiety, but again it has some feeling of certainty and safety about it.

It may take a long time for you to become fully aware of this factor of resistance. Indeed you will resist becoming aware of it. (You may be already rebelling, as you read this!) There is such a desperate need to cling to the old way of life, the old emotional pattern, which is familiar, and the forces of resistance are very deep-rooted and subtle.

But you cannot have it both ways. You must make the choice. You can have the old negative, restricted life you have been living in recent years, or be prepared to accept new, positive goals of happiness and fulfilment. You can stay in the dark tunnel of your fear and frustration. But there is light at the end of the tunnel and *you can decide* to follow that light into the open, to a life of freedom and greater joy than you have known for many a year. Do I hear you saying: 'I haven't the courage'? That is the voice of resistance, of your unconscious saboteur! Be *wholly determined* to go forward, and then you will find the courage to take the first step.

12.

WHAT ABOUT MY CHILDREN?

Many agoraphobic mothers are concerned, and rightly so, about the effects of their own troubles on their children. The two questions uppermost in their minds are (i) the incidence of agoraphobia in families and (ii) the problems of children growing up with an agoraphobic mother.

The Question of Heredity
In his book *Fears and Phobias*, Dr Isaac Marks [1] has said: 'There is no firm evidence that genetic inheritance plays a significant part in the development of phobic states in particular patients.' He goes on to report that in a survey of phobic patients 19 per cent of agoraphobics reported that they had a close relative with the same kind of phobia: not a large percentage.

I think there is little doubt that the child's early environment is a more important factor than heredity as such. A child is so easily influenced by the attitudes of his mother, and if she is nervous and frightened out of doors (or in), the child will probably acquire the same feeling.

I am not a child psychiatrist, however; nor is my concern limited to the possibility of your child *becoming agoraphobic*. As a practising psychotherapist, I am thinking about his or her, general emotional stability. For the children of today may

[1] Marks, Dr Isaac. *Fears and Phobias*, Heinemann Medical Books, London.

become the patients of tomorrow, if their early environment is not helpful.

Practical Issues

Leaving aside the question of genetic factors, the importance of which is not yet established, how far is it likely that a mother's phobia will affect her children? I think the answer depends on many different factors.

Some mothers can accompany their families on at least some outings. For others who cannot leave the house at all, the position is much more difficult. In the latter case, it will be helpful if there are older children who are willing and able to take the younger ones out. If their father is good with the children, and is able to go out with them and join in their fun, it will be easier for them than if he is tied up with business affairs for long hours, or if he finds it difficult to identify himself with their needs.

If the mother is widowed, or separated from her husband, so that she has the sole care of the children, the problem will be greater still.

The family may live in a house with a garden, where the children can get plenty of fresh air and sunshine; this is obviously better for both their health and their spirits than if they are cooped up in a sky-scraper block of flats, with few facilities near at hand.

If there are grandparents or other relatives living close by, so that the youngsters can visit them on occasions, or if such relatives can have them for holidays, this will be a boon.

The Vital Factor

I do want to emphasize, however, that it is not the practical issues which are the most important, by any means. The lack of outings and holidays is something that a child will get over. But earlier in this book I discussed one factor which is vital in any child's emotional development — *relationship*. You may find this some consolation if you have been feeling guilty about your children missing some treats which others get.

It must also be a challenge — especially if you are one of those unfortunate victims caught up in a general anxiety state, and have become withdrawn and unable to rouse yourself to take much interest in other people's affairs. You *must* be genuinely interested in your chilren's lives if you are to be a real mother to them.

Remember, that little things mean a lot to children. Matters which seem trivial to you will loom large in their lives. It is important for you to bear this in mind, for you may be so devastated by your own problems that you feel other people's troubles are as nothing compared with yours. This will not be helpful where a child is involved.

Security

One of the deepest needs which your relationship should meet is that of security. You may have difficulties here. If you are holding your baby in your arms while you are petrified with fear yourself, or even feeling nervy and edgy, your child will sense your fear, and react in the same way. He will feel insecure.

Another facet of this problem arises where the atmosphere in the home has become strained, for no child feels secure if the relationship on which the home has been founded is uncertain.

Most children run to mother for safety if they are frightened; yours will look to *you* to be their tower of strength. This will demand a lot from you, but if you can concentrate on giving your little ones the love and security they need, you may well find your own troubles receding. Your concern for them will help to take your mind off your own fears.

Above all it is the security of your *love* which they need. A warm, tender, yet non-possessive relationship is the most precious thing you can offer them in the first few years of their life. They can survive a lot of disadvantages if they have this one 'pearl of great price'. In this lies your vocation as a mother, and in fulfilling it you will find that your own life is greatly enriched.

Some General Advice

If you already have children, let them go out as much as possible; encourage them to be independent. Conceal your own fears from them if you possibly can, or they will tend to adopt your own attitudes. Avoid *at all costs* the temptation to lean on them for company, no matter how hard this is for you.

Remember it is not always easy to assess what is going on in a child's emotions. If there are outward signs of distress or upset, like persistent bed-wetting, tantrums, stealing and so on, then you know something is wrong. Unfortunately the reverse is not so certain: a child may appear to be quite unaffected by factors in his early environment, but then in adolescence or later life he can be overcome by feelings of inadequacy, fears, or other emotional disorders which are traced to infant insecurity.

Perhaps you are considering the advisability or otherwise of having a child, and wondering whether or not this would help you to overcome your phobia.

There are patients who have *become* agoraphobic after childbirth; there are others whose phobic troubles have greatly improved after the birth of another child.

One thing is important: do not have a child *for the purpose* of helping you out of your troubles. This would be wrong. One sometimes hears it said: 'I think a baby would help us to hold our marriage together' or 'I think it's a good idea to have a child in later life: it helps to keep you young.' Do not adopt this kind of attitude in regard to your own problems. It is quite wrong to have a child with the unconscious expectation that the baby will do anything at all *for you*. One cannot and must not put any 'responsibility' on to a baby. If things do not turn out as you had hoped (if, in your case, your agoraphobia persists) you will be resentful. You may find the child a burden, without the advantage you hoped to get in compensation.

If you think of having children, do so only because of the joy you will know in expressing your love in this way, and the delight of seeing them grow up happy and independent. Your motive must be, in other words, an 'out-going' one.

Lastly, do not limit your thinking to the problem of whether your children will be affected by your phobia. Look forward, instead, to your emancipation. Your children cannot cure your phobia, but they can give you the necessary incentive so that *for their sakes* and your own, you explore every avenue open to you in a determined effort to find release.

13.

OVER TO YOU

There is one more thing I want to say to you, if you suffer from agoraphobia. It is this: you may be somewhat disappointed that this book has offered no easy solution, no ready answer which can put you out of your misery right away. You secretly look for a 'magic formula' which will eradicate your panic and fear in a flash. It is a very natural wish.

Your Responsibility
In my previous work as a college lecturer, sometimes a student would ask me at the outset of the course how many of my students passed the examination in the previous year! He was assessing my capabilities — which is fair enough — but there was also the suggestion that his success depended on me, rather than on himself. Naturally it was my responsibility to do all in my power to help and guide him in his study, but one cannot 'inject' knowledge: ultimately the student's own work and determination are necessary for success.

It is the same with emotional problems. Unfortunately it is not possible to obtain an injection of 'instant courage'. Nor is it possible to get rid of panic like one gets rid of an aching tooth — in one short, sharp operation.

A surgeon can remove a troublesome appendix without a great deal of help from you — all he needs is your signature on the consent form for the anaesthetic. If psychotherapy could be administered in the same way, how much easier it would be! But here the personality is involved — and that means your own will, your own brave, honest attempt to face up to your problems and weaknesses.

However many books you read, however many people you contact for advice, if you are putting the responsibility for a 'cure' on to someone else you will be disappointed, and possibly bitter.

'Nobody Understands'

One of the complaints of agoraphobics, as I have mentioned before, is that 'nobody understands'. This is one grievance to which you may turn time and time again, when really what you are doing is evading the issue. If some suggestion made to you is uncongenial, if the task seems too heavy, the challenge too great, you may well be tempted to shelter behind that well-worn phrase 'You don't understand'. You can go on like this for ever.

Indeed the lack of understanding can actually become 'libidinized' — by which I mean that you can actually live on your martyrdom; you can make a meal of it.

You may even be seething with indignation as you are reading this chapter. At least, you hoped, here would be one person who would know how helpless you are to help yourself. I know how you feel. I do understand how hard it is for you to believe that there is, in fact, anything you can do to help yourself. How easy it is for someone else to tell you what to do!

The First Move

I do wish I had an easier solution to offer to you. But there is none that I know of. You will have to accept the fact that if you are looking to someone else to help you out of your slough of despond without any real initiative on your part, then you are asking the impossible. It is like trying to lift someone who is physically unable to help himself. When the patient is a dead weight there is so little you can do; and if he can give no co-operation, when you cease to support him he falls back where he was before.

Courage is required to accept the fact that *you and you alone* can ultimately *ensure* your cure. If you have not the courage to face *that* fact, then you must accept the fact that you will spend the rest of your days in your old familiar prison.

If you do seek help from any source — your doctor, a

therapist, a phobics society, a friend — *you* have to play the
game. And the ball is in your court: the first move is yours.
At the end of the day, however, there is a prize to be won, and
what a worth-while one it is! I cannot give you 'instant courage',
but I can give you my understanding, and encouragement to
take the first step.

In Chapter Ten I told you of Mrs A., the widow who, after
eleven years of being confined to the house, made a brave
attempt to visit a former foster-child, and came back alone by
bus. Her article ended with these words: 'The only thing that
maddens me is that I did not try years ago.' Will that be *your*
regret in several years' time? I sincerely hope not.

Conclusion

Agoraphobia is distressing, debilitating and depressing. You
long for freedom, fulfilment and fun. Is it really possible to
achieve the transformation? Can agoraphobia *really* be cured?
The answer to that is 'yes' — if you really want to do it.

I have not suggested that the path is easy. It will take time
to change the emotional habits of several years. But it can be
done.

You, as the sufferer, know to what extent your own problem
restricts and embarrasses you. You alone know what you
expect from a cure. If your sole aim is to be free to go out,
to go on holidays, etc., then some course of desensitization
should help you enormously. Your own doctor will no doubt
be able to tell you the nearest hospital where you can obtain
such treatment, or there may be a psychotherapist in your area
who can help you. If it is quite impossible for you to get to
a trained therapist, then you can do a lot to help yourself, as
suggested in Chapter Ten. There are scores of people who can
vouch for the release that this type of therapy affords. It has
helped others, and it can help you, if you have the same
determination.

But you must make the first move. No one ever crossed the
ocean without leaving the shore; and no one ever crossed the
threshold without opening the door. That first, positive step
is so very important.

Remember that the weakness you feel is not so much physical
as emotional. By that I mean that it is your emotional state which
is producing the physical symptoms. But remember, too, that
the longer you stay put in your home, refusing to leave the

house, the weaker your legs are going to feel. If you have not been getting normal exercise your muscles will probably have become a little flabby.

Of course you feel strange at first. You may know from experience that a patient who comes home after a long stay in hospital feels quite odd at first in the outside world. Indeed, I remember that after a six months' stay in hospital I myself felt *terribly* strange, even in the living room of my own home. Can you wonder that after being in the house for so long — years perhaps — you feel strange and somewhat at a loss when you venture into the street?

Do not be misled into thinking this feeling is some sort of illness or terrible cause for alarm. It will take time for you to re-orientate yourself in the world of cars and buses, or crowded supermarkets and open parks, from which you have withdrawn yourself for so long.

Every day you put it off, the more difficult it will become for you to make the effort. But your recovery lies, not in thinking and wondering and wishing, but in *doing* — in taking that first positive step.

Some of you who read this book will recognize that merely to go out freely again is not the answer to the deepest needs of your own personality. You know that there are other factors which are robbing you of your true potential. You will only be satisfied if you can get to the *source* of the trouble and put that right.

Treating a sick plant is all very well. But if something is eating at the root, or if it is growing in the wrong soil, the plant will be weak, however much it is treated on the surface. Likewise if jealousy, frustration, bitterness or guilt is eating at the root of your emotional life, then your personality is being impaired. Or if, unfortunately, the environment in which you spent your earliest years failed to provide the right conditions for healthy, stable emotional development, then the 'soil' needs changing. You need to make a fresh start, to grow up again emotionally, in an atmosphere of security and self-acceptance, so that you acquire a positive and fulfilling philosophy of life.

Analytic therapy, where it is available, can provide the answer for those who prefer this more radical approach to their problem. But psychotherapy, too, can be painful. To live again through one's fears and insecurity, in order to understand them and find freedom from them, does take courage. But only those who have gone that way, and found complete release from their problem know what it means to become a new person. The cathartic nature of such an experience cannot be denied. It makes for wholeness and maturity of personality.

To be, or not to be? That is the question! The choice is yours. Only you can make the decision. No one can force you to do anything you do not wish to do, and without your own determination and co-operation *any* therapist is helpless.

You can remain in your prison, with your fears, and with all the worry and distress and frustration which is entailed for you and your family. Or you can go forward, knowing that *there is a way through your fear, to freedom and to fulfilment.*

USEFUL ADDRESSES

The Phobics Society
4 Cheltenham Road
Chorlton-cum-Hardy
Manchester
M21 1QN
(President: Katharine Fisher)

The Open Door Association
447 Pensby Road
Heswall
Wirral
Merseyside
L61 9PQ
(National Organizer: Mona Woodford)

Phobias Confidential
1 Clovelly Road
Ealing
London
W5 5HF

Nottingham and County Phobic Association
1 Oban Road
Chilwell
Nottingham
(Founder President: Tony Elliott)

Horizon
Pam Moscrop
244 Whickham View
Denton Burn
Newcastle-upon-Tyne

Out and About Association
Morny Murrihy
St John's House
Seafield Road
Clontarf
Dublin 3
Eire

Dr Claire Weekes's cassettes and records are available from:

16 Rivermead Court
Ranelagh Gardens
London
SW6 3RT

or from The Open Door Association.

FURTHER READING

Bailes, Frederick. *Your Mind Can Heal You*, Allen & Unwin, London, 1969.

Barker, C. Edward. *Nerves and Their Cure*, Allen & Unwin, London, 1968.

Guntrip, Harry S. *Your Mind and Your Health*, Unwin Books, London, 1970.

Northfield, Wilfrid. *How to Relax*, Thorsons, Wellingborough, 1977.

Vose, Ruth Hurst. *Agoraphobia*, Faber, London, 1981.

Weekes, Dr Claire. *Peace from Nervous Suffering*, Angus & Robertson, London, 1981.

Weekes, Dr Claire. *Agoraphobia*, Angus & Robertson, London, 1977.

INDEX

Acupuncture, 49
Aggressiveness, 23-24
Agoraphobia
  causes of, 26-29, 39-38
  definition of, 16
  difficulty in understanding, 9-10,
    15-16, 23-24, 27-28, 29, 87
  and the family, 9-10, 23-24, 32,
    82-85
  prevalence of, 16-20
  sensitization, 26-28, 30-31
  sex distribution, 18-19
  symptoms, 16-17, 21-25
'Association' (in psychotherapy), 63,
  75-76
Auto-suggestion, 49

Childhood, 32-36, 39-41, 52,
  63-64, 76, 78-79, 82
Contextual therapy, 55

Dependence, 33-34, 39, 41, 60-61,
  80
Desensitization, 53-55, 58-59, 60,
  63, 66-70, 77, 88
Doormat personality, 32, 37-38
Dreams, 41, 62-63

Drugs, 51

Ego-weakness, 36, 42, 60, 62, 80

Fear
  living through it, 48-49, 54-56,
    67, 70-73, 89
  of fainting, 37
  of freedom, 36, 41
  of panic, 18, 29, 31, 60
  of the street, 16-17, 29, 36, 42,
    43, 79
Flooding, 55, 71
Freud, Sigmund, 34, 35

Group therapy, 56
Guilt, 23-24, 27, 34-38, 60, 63, 64,
  80
Guntrip, Harry S., 41, 42, 43

Heredity, 82
Hypnotherapy, 50

Indecision, 22, 42
Institute for Neuro-physiological
  Psychology, 30-31
Intolerance, 24-25

Isolation dread, 42-43

Open Door, the, 10-11, 24-25, 50
Open Spaces, 24-25, 76
Organic brain dysfunction (OBD),
    30-31

Phobics Society, The, 11
Psychotherapy, 31, 58, 60-61,
    62-65, 86, 89

Relationships
  effects of agoraphobia on, 24
  as factor underlying
    agoraphobia, 32-36, 37-38, 65
  as factor in therapy, 64
  in infancy, 32-33, 35, 40-41,
    83-84
Relaxation, 54, 55, 62, 67-69,
    72-73, 75

Religious faith, 47-48
Repression, 32, 34, 77, 78
Resistance, 63, 74, 78-81

Schizoid state, 40-42, 44
Security, 34, 64-65, 84, 89
    false, 79
Separation anxiety, 33, 52
Sexual problems, 19, 36-37, 65
'Shock therapy' (ECT), 49-50
Spiritual healing, 47-48

Tension, 22, 24, 28, 34
Trapped, feeling of being, 17, 32,
    36, 38, 40, 41, 42, 43, 76

Unconscious, 34, 59, 77, 78, 80
Unreality, 22, 43-44

Weekes, Claire, 58, 66-67